MONEY LESSONS FOR MILITARY FAMILIES

Managing Frequent Moves, Deployments, and Unique Benefits

Mitchell C. Henderson

Money Lessons for Military Families: Managing Frequent Moves, Deployments, and Unique Benefits

Copyright © 2024

All rights reserved.
No part of this book may be reproduced in any form without permission, except brief quotations for review purposes.

ISBN: 9798305379792

Disclaimer:
This book is for educational and motivational purposes only. It does not constitute financial advice. Readers should consult a qualified financial advisor before making financial decisions.

*This book is dedicated to
all of our soldiers.*

Contents

Introduction: Navigating Financial Life as a Military Family	7
Chapter 1: The Financial Realities of Military Life	9
Chapter 2: Military Pay and Benefits Demystified	14
Chapter 3: Setting Financial Goals as a Military Family	20
Chapter 4: Building a Flexible Budget	26
Chapter 5: Emergency Funds for the Unexpected	33
Chapter 6: Maximizing Military Discounts and Resources	40
Chapter 7: Renting vs. Buying with Frequent Moves	48
Chapter 8: PCS (Permanent Change of Station) Planning	56
Chapter 9: Protecting Your Assets During Employments	64
Chapter 10: Retirement Planning with the TSP	72
Chapter 11: Investing for Military Families	80
Chapter 12: Building Passive Income Streams	88
Chapter 13: Transitioning to Civilian Life	96
Chapter 14: Education and Career Benefits for Families	105
Chapter 15: Creating a Legacy for Future Generations	112
Chapter 16: Thriving Despite Challenges	120
Chapter 17: Building a Supportive Community	126
Chapter 18: Celebrating Progress and Adjusting Goals	132
Conclusion: A Financially Strong Military Family	138

Introduction
Navigating Financial Life as a Military Family

Military life is unique, challenging, and often unpredictable. From frequent moves to deployments, life in the service demands flexibility, resilience, and strategic planning. But while these challenges are significant, they also come with opportunities—especially when it comes to your financial future.

For military families, financial literacy isn't just a skill—it's a lifeline. With the right knowledge and tools, you can turn the challenges of military life into stepping stones for building wealth, stability, and a lasting legacy. Whether you're preparing for a Permanent Change of Station (PCS), navigating the complexities of the Thrift Savings Plan (TSP), or transitioning to civilian life, every step offers a chance to take control of your financial destiny.

This book is designed to help you do just that. We'll dive into the unique financial realities of military life, break down the benefits and resources available to you, and provide practical strategies to thrive no matter where you're stationed or what circumstances you face. Our goal is to equip you with actionable advice tailored to the military lifestyle, empowering you to make the most of your hard-earned income and benefits.

Here's the truth: military families can build wealth and financial security, but it requires intentional planning and the right mindset. This book will help you identify opportunities, navigate obstacles, and build a financial foundation that supports your family's goals—whether you're serving now or preparing for life after service.

We'll also challenge you to dream bigger. Financial stability isn't just about balancing budgets or cutting expenses; it's about creating a vision for your family's future and taking consistent steps to achieve it.

This isn't just a book of financial tips—it's a guide to thriving in the face of uncertainty and creating a legacy for generations to come. Together, we'll explore how to adapt your financial goals to a mobile lifestyle, make the most of the benefits you've earned, and turn challenges into opportunities for growth.

Whether you're just starting your journey in the military or have years of service behind you, this book is your roadmap to financial success. Let's get started. Your future is waiting.

Chapter 1
The Financial Realities of Military Life

Military life is unlike any other, and when it comes to finances, it comes with its own set of challenges and rewards. From moving every few years to adjusting to unpredictable deployments, military families are accustomed to navigating transitions—often with little notice. While these changes can be daunting, they also present unique opportunities for growth, both personally and financially.

The Challenges You Face

Frequent moves are perhaps one of the most defining aspects of military life. Each Permanent Change of Station (PCS) brings new challenges—new housing markets, fluctuating costs of living, and the stress of adjusting to unfamiliar places. Add to that the complexities of deployments, where one partner might be absent for months or even longer, and the financial juggling act becomes even more intense.

Career transitions are another key challenge. Whether you're navigating a change in rank, a move to a new branch of the military, or even thinking about your future beyond service, these transitions can impact your income, your benefits, and your long-term financial goals.

However, these challenges aren't insurmountable. With the right mindset and a strategic approach, military families can thrive financially, even in the face of these uncertainties.

Understanding Military Pay and Benefits

One of the first steps in managing your finances as a military family is understanding the pay structure and the unique benefits available to you. Military compensation is unlike traditional civilian pay, with a combination of base pay, allowances, and special benefits that require careful planning to optimize.

- **Base Pay:** This is the foundation of your income, determined by your rank and years of service. While base pay is predictable, it can fluctuate with promotions, raises, or career changes.

- **Allowances:** Military families often receive allowances like the **Basic Allowance for Housing (BAH), Cost of Living Allowance (COLA)**, and **Family Separation Allowance (FSA)**. These allowances are designed to offset the costs of living and moving, but they vary depending on location and circumstances. Properly understanding these allowances and factoring them into your budget is essential.

- **Special Pays and Bonuses:** Whether it's a deployment bonus, hazardous duty pay, or other special allowances, these add to your overall compensation but can also be temporary. It's important to distinguish between regular income and these variable earnings.

The key to managing military pay and benefits effectively is creating a flexible budget that accounts for these differences. You'll need to track your income carefully and adjust as necessary—especially when moving to a new duty station or receiving special pays.

Budgeting for a Dynamic Life

In the military, "predictable" might not always be the word you'd use to describe life, but "adaptable" should be. That's why a good budget isn't just about tracking what you earn, but about preparing for the unknown.

As we'll explore later in this book, a flexible budget that can accommodate frequent moves, deployments, and other shifts in income is essential. You can't always predict how much you'll need to spend on housing or utilities, but with careful planning, you can ensure that you stay ahead of the game, no matter what life throws your way.

Exercise: Create a Basic Snapshot of Your Current Financial Situation

Before diving into deeper strategies, let's start with a clear understanding of where you stand financially. This exercise will help you build a snapshot of your current financial picture and serve as a baseline for future progress.

1. **List Your Income Sources**
    - Base Pay: _____
    - BAH (Basic Allowance for Housing): _____
    - COLA (Cost of Living Allowance): _____
    - Other Allowances or Special Pays: _____
    - Other Sources of Income: _____

2. **Track Your Expenses** Take a few moments to write down your current monthly expenses. This includes rent or mortgage, utilities, groceries, insurance, transportation, child care, and any other recurring costs. Try to be as thorough as possible, as this will give you a clearer picture of your financial habits.

3. **Assess Your Savings and Investments**

- Emergency Fund: _____
- Retirement Savings (TSP or Other): _____
- Investment Accounts: _____
- Other Assets: _____

4. **Debt Snapshot**
   - Credit Card Debt: _____
   - Car Loans: _____
   - Student Loans: _____
   - Other Debts: _____

By taking the time to assess your current financial situation, you'll be able to see where you stand today and where there's room for improvement. Remember, the goal is to build a solid foundation that can weather any storm—whether it's a PCS, a deployment, or a career transition.

This is just the beginning, but knowing where you are now is the first step in transforming your financial future. Let's keep moving forward, one step at a time!

Chapter 2
Military Pay and Benefits Demystified

Military pay can seem complex, but once you understand how it works, it becomes a powerful tool for building financial security. From base pay to allowances, benefits, and retirement savings, the military offers a range of financial opportunities that, when leveraged properly, can set you on the path to wealth and long-term stability.

In this chapter, we'll break down the key components of military pay and benefits, focusing on how to maximize each one. Whether you're just starting out in the military or looking for ways to optimize your current compensation, understanding these elements is crucial for making the most of your finances.

The Basics of Military Pay

Your military pay is made up of several different components. At the core, you have your **base pay**, which is determined by your rank and years of service. But beyond base pay, there are additional benefits that help offset the cost of military life—especially given the frequent moves and deployments you may experience. These benefits can significantly impact your overall financial picture, so it's important to understand them and factor them into your budget.

- **Basic Allowance for Housing (BAH):** BAH is one of the most significant benefits military families receive. It's designed to help cover the cost of housing, and it varies based on location, rank, and whether you have dependents. Unlike rent or mortgage payments, BAH is a tax-free allowance that gives you flexibility when it comes to where you live. Understanding how your BAH is calculated and how it varies by duty station is key to planning your housing and overall budget.

- **Cost of Living Allowance (COLA):** COLA helps to offset the difference in the cost of living between various duty stations, especially when stationed overseas or in high-cost areas. If you're moving to a location with a higher cost of living, COLA ensures you're not financially burdened by the price hike. It's important to check the current COLA rate for your duty station to see how it impacts your income.

- **Other Perks and Allowances:** Beyond BAH and COLA, there are a number of other allowances and benefits that can ease your financial load, such as the **Family Separation Allowance (FSA)** during deployments, the **Uniform Allowance**, and **Hazardous Duty Pay**. These benefits are designed to support military families during unique circumstances, and you should always be aware of any additional pay you qualify for based on your assignments.

The Thrift Savings Plan (TSP): A Powerful Tool for Retirement Savings

As a military member, you have access to one of the most valuable retirement savings vehicles available: the **Thrift Savings Plan (TSP)**. The TSP allows you to save for retirement in a tax-advantaged way, and it offers an array of investment options to grow your savings over time.

- **Why the TSP Matters:** Whether you're in the **Blended Retirement System (BRS)** or the **Legacy Retirement System**, the TSP is a critical tool for your financial future. Not only do you contribute to your TSP, but if you're under BRS, the military will match your contributions up to a certain point, giving you "free" money toward your retirement.

- **Contribution Limits:** In 2024, service members can contribute up to $22,500 a year to their TSP ($30,000 if you're age 50 or older). The beauty of the TSP is that you can choose between **traditional contributions** (tax-deferred) or **Roth contributions** (tax-free growth), depending on your tax strategy and future income expectations.

- **Investment Options:** The TSP offers a range of investment options, including low-cost index funds that track major U.S. stock markets, bonds, and government securities. You can tailor your TSP investments based on your risk tolerance and retirement timeline. It's essential to start contributing to the TSP as early as possible to take full advantage of compound growth.

Exercise: Review Your LES (Leave and Earnings Statement) to Identify All Available Benefits

Your **Leave and Earnings Statement (LES)** is the most important document for understanding your military pay and benefits. Every month, it provides a detailed breakdown of your earnings, deductions, and available allowances. By reviewing your LES regularly, you can ensure that you're maximizing all of your benefits and make informed decisions about budgeting and saving.

1. **Identify Your Base Pay** Look at your base pay and determine how it compares to your current

living expenses. Is it sufficient to cover your essential needs? If not, consider how you can adjust your budget or take advantage of available allowances.

2. **Check Your BAH and COLA** Review your Basic Allowance for Housing (BAH) and Cost of Living Allowance (COLA). Are these allowances meeting your housing needs? If you're stationed at a high-cost location, are there other resources to help manage these costs?

3. **Look for Additional Allowances and Benefits** Search for any special pays or bonuses that may apply to your current situation—such as Family Separation Allowance (FSA), Hazardous Duty Pay, or other benefits. Make sure that you're receiving all the financial support you're entitled to.

4. **Check Your TSP Contributions** Review your TSP contributions and consider increasing them, especially if you're eligible for the military match. Remember, even small increases can have a significant impact on your long-term retirement savings.

By completing this exercise, you'll gain a clearer understanding of your current financial situation and be empowered to make smarter, more informed decisions moving forward.

Understanding military pay and benefits is the first step in taking control of your financial future. Armed with this knowledge, you can maximize your compensation, set up a solid savings plan, and ensure that your family is on the path to financial security—no matter where your military journey takes you.

Chapter 3
Setting Financial Goals as a Military Family

Financial goals are your roadmap to a secure and prosperous future. Without them, it's easy to drift through life, responding to immediate needs and never fully realizing the financial freedom you deserve. But with clear goals, you gain a sense of purpose, direction, and motivation to take control of your finances, even when life's challenges seem overwhelming.

As a military family, your financial journey is unique. The unpredictability of frequent moves, deployments, and career transitions can make long-term planning seem like an uphill battle. However, this doesn't mean you can't set—and achieve—meaningful financial goals. In fact, the very nature of military life offers an opportunity to refine your planning skills and adapt to changing circumstances, all while securing a stable financial future.

In this chapter, we'll dive into the importance of setting both short-term and long-term financial goals, and how you can adapt these goals to the dynamic nature of military life. By the end, you'll have a personalized set of financial objectives that are aligned with your family's needs, helping you build the life you've always dreamed of.

The Importance of Short-Term and Long-Term Financial Planning

Setting financial goals isn't just about knowing where you want to be in the future; it's about making daily, intentional choices that lead you there. For military families, this means balancing the immediate needs of today with the long-term vision of tomorrow.

- **Short-Term Financial Goals** Short-term goals are those that you can achieve in the near future—within the next 6 to 12 months. These goals address immediate concerns and give you quick wins that build momentum. For example, setting a goal to create a budget, build an emergency fund, or pay off credit card debt are excellent short-term goals. They provide financial stability, reduce stress, and set the foundation for more ambitious plans.

- **Long-Term Financial Goals** Long-term goals are those that take more time to achieve—often 3, 5, or even 10 years or more. These are your "big picture" goals, such as saving for retirement, buying a home, or paying off student loans. Achieving long-term goals requires patience and consistency, but it's these types of goals that truly lead to financial freedom and generational wealth.

In the military, long-term goals may feel a bit more daunting due to the constant changes in assignments, relocations, and career progression. But with a clear plan, flexibility, and determination, these goals are entirely attainable.

Adapting Financial Goals to the Unpredictability of Military Life

Military life is inherently unpredictable—whether it's a sudden move, an unexpected deployment, or a shift in your spouse's military career. Yet, this unpredictability can be managed by setting adaptable goals that take life's twists and turns into account.

- **Embrace Flexibility:** Your goals should be strong enough to withstand disruptions, but flexible enough to adapt when things change. For example, you may need to adjust your timeline for buying a home due to a sudden PCS move, or rework your budget if your family faces a temporary loss of income during deployment. Flexibility allows you to maintain focus without getting discouraged when life throws you a curveball.

- **Leverage Resources:** The military offers a range of resources that can help you achieve your financial goals, from financial counseling services to special allowances and benefits. Incorporating these resources into your goals can accelerate your progress and provide valuable support when times are tough.

- **Focus on What You Can Control:** You may not have control over when you're moved or deployed, but you can control how you manage your money, prioritize savings, and make the most of the opportunities in front of you. Keep your goals centered on areas where you have control, and be proactive in shaping your financial future.

Exercise: Write Down Three Financial Goals Tailored to Your Family's Needs

Now it's time to take action. To build a solid foundation for your financial future, you need to identify specific goals that are meaningful to your family. Write down at least three financial goals that are tailored to your current situation and military lifestyle.

Here are a few examples to inspire you:

1. **Short-Term Goal (3-6 months):**
   "Build an emergency fund of $1,000 to cover unexpected expenses, such as car repairs or medical bills."

   - This goal provides immediate financial security, which is essential when the unexpected happens.

2. **Medium-Term Goal (1-2 years):**
   "Pay off $5,000 in credit card debt or personal loans to reduce monthly payments and free up money for other financial priorities."

   - Eliminating high-interest debt is a critical step toward financial freedom and enables you to focus on savings and investing.

3. **Long-Term Goal (3-5 years):**
   "Save for a down payment on a home, aiming for 20% of the purchase price."

   - With the military's moving schedule, it's common to rent, but owning a home can be a smart long-term investment for building wealth. This goal gives you something to work toward, even if it needs to be adjusted based on PCS orders.

Remember: These are just examples—your goals should reflect what's most important to your family. Perhaps your goals involve funding your children's education, setting up a retirement fund, or paying off a vehicle loan. Whatever they are, make sure they are specific, measurable, and time-bound.

Action Steps:

1. Take a moment to think about where you are financially right now. What challenges are you facing? What opportunities do you have ahead?
2. Write down three financial goals that reflect your current priorities, making sure they're SMART (Specific, Measurable, Achievable, Relevant, Time-bound).
3. Break each goal down into actionable steps, and determine how you can stay flexible if circumstances change.

By the end of this exercise, you'll have a clear financial roadmap tailored to your unique needs as a military family. And remember, your goals can—and will—evolve over time. The important part is that you have a vision for the future and a plan to make it happen. Keep moving forward, stay committed to your goals, and embrace the journey ahead.

Chapter 4
Building a Flexible Budget

A budget isn't just a list of numbers—it's the foundation that supports the financial freedom you're working toward. For military families, building a budget goes beyond tracking where your money goes each month. It's about creating a plan that works *for* you, even when life throws its curveballs. Frequent moves, changing pay rates, fluctuating expenses, and the unpredictability of military life can all make budgeting feel like a moving target. But with the right tools and mindset, you can create a budget that adapts to your lifestyle, helping you stay on track no matter what comes your way.

In this chapter, we'll show you how to build a flexible budget that allows for the unique challenges of military life—whether you're navigating a new base, dealing with unexpected deployment expenses, or planning for the next PCS move. By the end, you'll have a budgeting plan that helps you thrive, no matter how often your situation changes.

Creating a Budget That Accommodates Frequent Moves and Changing Expenses

Military families are no strangers to the unpredictability of life. PCS orders can arrive at a moment's notice, deployments can alter financial plans, and housing expenses can vary greatly depending on your location. So, how can you create a budget that remains effective despite all this change?

- **Anticipate and Adjust for Moving Costs:** Moving can be expensive, but it's something every military family can expect at some point. From shipping household goods to setting up utilities, moving costs can quickly add up. A flexible budget accounts for this by saving in advance for relocation-related expenses and tracking reimbursements from the military. Setting aside a specific fund for moves ensures that unexpected costs don't throw off your entire financial plan.

- **Factor in Changing Housing Costs:** Housing is often one of the most significant expenses for military families. Depending on where you're stationed, your BAH (Basic Allowance for Housing) may cover your rent, or you may need to supplement it. Housing allowances can vary, so it's important to budget accordingly and adjust for potential increases or decreases in rent. A flexible budget gives you the wiggle room you need to accommodate these changes without sacrificing other financial priorities.

- **Track Irregular Expenses:** With the unpredictable nature of military life, there are always some expenses that can't be predicted—a vehicle breakdown, unexpected medical bills, or a last-minute trip home for a family emergency. To manage these irregular costs, you should build a "buffer" into your budget. This could be a small percentage of your income that's set aside for the unexpected, so when things don't go as planned, you have the financial flexibility to handle them.

Managing Fluctuating Housing and Utility Costs

One of the most significant challenges of military life is the fluctuation in housing and utility costs. The BAH you receive may or may not cover your full rent, and utilities can vary widely depending on location. While military families are often provided with housing allowances, the goal is to use them wisely and minimize out-of-pocket expenses.

- **Housing Allowance and Rent Adjustments:** It's essential to understand your BAH and how it aligns with your local housing market. If your rent exceeds your BAH, you'll need to account for the difference in your budget. On the other hand, if your BAH exceeds the rent, you can save the surplus or use it for other financial goals. This flexibility is key to maintaining balance when your housing costs fluctuate.

- **Utility Costs:** Utilities are another area where military families experience variability. In some areas, utilities are included in rent; in others, you're responsible for paying them separately. As a proactive step, reach out to the housing office or your landlord when you arrive at your new location to understand what's included in your rent and what's not. From there, you can build utilities into your budget to avoid surprises.

- **Energy-Efficient Practices:** Reducing energy consumption in your home can be a simple yet effective way to manage fluctuating utility costs. Adopting energy-efficient practices—like using LED bulbs, unplugging devices when not in use, and investing in a programmable thermostat—can help lower your monthly utility bills, providing a little more flexibility in your budget.

Exercise: Set Up a Budget Template with Room for Flexibility

Now it's time to put your knowledge into action! Below is a simple, customizable budget template designed with military families in mind. This template allows you to track your income, anticipate fluctuating expenses, and adjust for the unexpected.

1. **List Your Income**
   Start by listing all sources of income, including your basic pay, BAH, COLA (Cost of Living Allowance), any special pay, and other income sources (like a side hustle or a spouse's job).

   - Basic Pay: _____
   - BAH: _____
   - COLA: _____
   - Other: _____

2. **Track Your Fixed Expenses**
   These are the expenses that stay relatively stable each month, such as rent, utilities, and debt payments.

   - Rent/Mortgage: _____
   - Utilities (electricity, gas, water, etc.): _____
   - Insurance (health, auto, life, etc.): _____
   - Loan Payments (car, student loans, etc.): _____

3. **Plan for Variable Expenses**

   These are expenses that may fluctuate month-to-month, such as groceries, gas, and entertainment.

   - Groceries: _____
   - Gas/Transportation: _____
   - Entertainment: _____
   - Miscellaneous: _____

4. **Set Aside for Savings and Emergencies**

   This is where flexibility comes into play. Set aside a certain percentage of your income for savings, and always include a cushion for unexpected expenses.

   - Emergency Fund: _____
   - Retirement Savings (TSP, IRAs, etc.): _____
   - Short-Term Savings (vacation, special purchases, etc.): _____

5. **Account for PCS and Moving Expenses**

   Make sure to budget for any upcoming move or PCS. Consider expenses like travel, temporary lodging, and moving services.

   - PCS Fund: _____
   - Moving Expenses (gas, lodging, meals): _____

6. **Review and Adjust Monthly**

   At the end of each month, review your budget.

Were there any unexpected expenses? Did you get reimbursed for any PCS-related costs? Adjust your budget for the next month, ensuring that you stay on track with your savings and financial goals.

Action Steps:
1. Use the template provided to create your own flexible budget.
2. Make sure you account for any upcoming moves or PCS transitions by setting aside funds for those expenses.
3. Review your budget regularly and adjust as needed to stay on top of changes in your income and expenses.

Remember, the goal of a flexible budget isn't perfection—it's about making sure your finances align with your life's priorities. Military life can be unpredictable, but with a budget that adapts to your changing circumstances, you can stay in control of your financial future. Whether you're navigating a new base, preparing for a move, or planning for the future, your budget is the key to making it all work. Stay focused, stay flexible, and keep moving forward. You've got this!

Chapter 5
Emergency Funds for the Unexpected

Life in the military can be unpredictable. Between moves, deployments, and the unique challenges of military life, unexpected expenses are almost a certainty. Whether it's a sudden medical emergency, a broken-down car, or an unexpected PCS move that disrupts your finances, having a solid emergency fund is one of the most important steps you can take to secure your family's financial stability.

An emergency fund is your financial safety net, providing you with peace of mind and the ability to weather any storm without derailing your long-term financial goals. In this chapter, we'll show you why a robust emergency fund is so essential for military families and how to create and grow one, even when your budget feels tight.

Why Military Families Need an Emergency Fund

As a military family, you're no stranger to the unpredictability of life. Things can change in an instant—orders can come in for a new station, a vehicle might need repairs, or a spouse may need to suddenly travel for an emergency. The key to handling these disruptions with ease is having enough money set aside to cover the unexpected.

Military families face unique circumstances that make an emergency fund even more crucial:

- **Frequent Moves and PCS Costs:** Moving can be expensive, and sometimes the costs aren't fully covered by the military. A well-funded emergency fund allows you to cover moving expenses without racking up credit card debt.

- **Deployment or Separation:** If a spouse is deployed, managing finances can become more complicated. Having an emergency fund can help cover additional costs during this time.

- **Fluctuating Income:** With fluctuating pay, allowances, and changes in family size, it's essential to have a buffer to smooth out any gaps in your finances.

An emergency fund isn't just about handling financial stress—it's about protecting your peace of mind and maintaining stability during life's inevitable curveballs.

How to Save Despite Tight Budgets: Automating Savings and Cutting Unnecessary Expenses

For many military families, saving for an emergency fund can seem like an impossible task. You might feel that your budget is already stretched too thin. But no matter your financial situation, building an emergency fund is achievable—and it doesn't have to happen all at once.

- **Automate Your Savings:** One of the most effective ways to save, especially when things feel tight, is to automate the process. Set up automatic transfers from your checking account into your emergency savings account. Start with a small, manageable amount (even $25 or $50 a month), and gradually increase it as you can. The key is consistency.

- **Start Small, Think Big:** You don't need to save your entire emergency fund overnight. Aim for a smaller initial goal, like $500 or $1,000, and build from there. This small amount can cover many common emergencies, and once you reach that milestone, you'll feel motivated to keep growing it.

- **Cut Unnecessary Expenses:** If you're finding it hard to set aside money, it may be time to look at your spending habits. Take a close look at your monthly expenses and identify areas where you can cut back. Could you cancel a subscription you don't use? Reduce dining out or entertainment expenses? The key is to find small, sustainable ways to free up money for savings without sacrificing your overall well-being.

- **Use Windfalls Wisely:** Tax returns, bonuses, and other unexpected sources of income are great opportunities to boost your emergency fund. Instead of spending this money on non-essentials, consider funneling a portion of it into your emergency savings. This will help you reach your goal faster without straining your regular budget.

Exercise: Create a Plan to Build or Grow Your Emergency Fund

Now it's time to get practical! Use the following steps to create a plan that works for your family. Whether you're starting from scratch or growing an existing emergency fund, these steps will help you make progress toward a more financially secure future.

1. **Set Your Target Amount**

- The ideal emergency fund should cover three to six months of living expenses. However, if that feels overwhelming, start smaller. Consider an initial target of $500–$1,000 for minor emergencies, and work your way up from there.
- Target Amount: _____ (Your goal could be $500, $1,000, or more depending on your situation).

2. **Review Your Monthly Income and Expenses**

   - Take a look at your budget and see how much you can realistically set aside each month for your emergency fund. Even if you can only save $25–$50 a month, that's a great place to start.
   - Monthly Savings Target: _____

3. **Automate Your Savings**

   - Set up an automatic transfer from your checking account to your emergency savings account. Choose a date that works best for your pay schedule (right after you receive your pay is ideal).
   - Automation Setup: Have you set up an automatic transfer? YES / NO

4. **Cutting Unnecessary Expenses**

- Identify at least one area where you can reduce your spending each month. This could be cutting back on eating out, canceling subscriptions, or reducing impulse purchases.
- Expense to Cut Back On: _____

5. **Find Ways to Boost Your Fund**

    - Will you use tax returns, bonuses, or any extra income to boost your savings? If so, set aside a portion of this money for your emergency fund.
    - Windfall Income to Save: _____

6. **Monitor and Adjust**

    - Regularly review your progress and adjust as needed. If you're able to save more one month, increase your monthly savings target. If you're struggling, look for ways to cut additional costs.
    - Progress Review Date: _____

Remember, building an emergency fund isn't about perfection—it's about progress. The goal is to give yourself a financial cushion that allows you to handle the unexpected without derailing your plans. By taking small, consistent steps, you'll create a safety net that empowers you to navigate military life with confidence.

Action Steps:
1. Set a realistic savings goal for your emergency fund.
2. Review your budget and find a manageable amount to save each month.
3. Set up automatic transfers to your emergency fund account.
4. Cut back on unnecessary expenses to free up more money for savings.
5. Use windfall income to give your savings a boost.
6. Regularly monitor your progress and adjust your plan as needed.

With each deposit into your emergency fund, you're building resilience and peace of mind for your family. Life in the military can be unpredictable, but with an emergency fund in place, you'll be able to weather any storm with confidence. Keep moving forward—you've got this!

Chapter 6
Maximizing Military Discounts and Resources

As a military family, you have access to a wide array of discounts and resources designed to make life a little easier—and a lot more affordable. From shopping discounts to financial counseling services, the benefits available to you can make a significant difference in your budget, helping you stretch every dollar further. But many of these resources go underutilized simply because they're not always top of mind.

In this chapter, we'll explore how to maximize military discounts, take full advantage of commissaries, and tap into free financial counseling services. We'll also dive into some powerful programs like Military OneSource and the Armed Forces Relief Trust that offer support for everything from financial planning to family counseling. By using these resources to their fullest, you'll be able to save money, reduce stress, and secure a stronger financial foundation for your family.

Leveraging Military Discounts, Commissaries, and Free Financial Counseling Services

Military discounts are one of the easiest ways to save money, and they're available in a wide range of categories—whether it's shopping, dining, entertainment, or even travel. These discounts are your military family's secret weapon for cutting costs and building wealth. Here's how to make the most of them:

- **Retail Discounts:** Many national retailers offer military discounts, from clothing stores to tech retailers. Don't forget to ask! Some stores give discounts just for showing your military ID, while others require you to sign up for a military membership or use a special code. A few minutes of research can unlock a whole world of savings.

- **Dining Discounts:** Restaurants often offer military discounts, ranging from a small percentage off to free meals on special holidays like Memorial Day or Veterans Day. Make it a habit to ask about discounts whenever you dine out, and check online for listings of restaurants offering military deals.

- **Travel and Entertainment Discounts:** Whether you're booking a vacation or planning a weekend getaway, military families can access significant savings on hotels, flights, rental cars, and theme park tickets. Many companies partner with military organizations to offer discounts or special packages exclusively for military families.

- **Commissaries and Exchanges:** The commissary is your go-to spot for grocery shopping, offering food and household items at significant discounts compared to retail stores. The exchanges, which are like department stores, also offer reduced prices on clothing, electronics, and other items. Take advantage of these facilities to save on everyday necessities.

In addition to these discounts, there are several **free financial counseling services** available to military families. Programs like **Military OneSource** provide free, confidential financial counseling to help you plan for your future, manage debt, and navigate the complexities of military pay. Financial counselors can guide you through budgeting, saving, investing, and even retirement planning, giving you the tools to take control of your finances.

Programs Like Military OneSource and Armed Forces Relief Trust

Military OneSource is a comprehensive resource that provides a wealth of support for active-duty service members and their families. This service offers more than just financial counseling—it's a one-stop-shop for all things military family-related. Here's how you can use Military OneSource to your advantage:

- **Financial Counseling and Education:** Military OneSource provides free access to certified financial planners who can assist with everything from creating a budget to managing debt. They can help you navigate military benefits, set financial goals, and even provide advice on how to make the most of your Thrift Savings Plan (TSP).

- **Legal Assistance:** In addition to financial counseling, Military OneSource offers access to free legal consultations for issues like estate planning, family law, and debt management. Legal experts can help you understand military laws and provide peace of mind in handling any legal matters.

- **Career Counseling and Support:** For spouses transitioning into civilian careers or looking for new opportunities, Military OneSource also offers career counseling. This includes resume reviews, job search support, and advice on leveraging military benefits for education and training.

Another valuable resource is the **Armed Forces Relief Trust (AFRT)**, a nonprofit organization dedicated to supporting military families in need. The AFRT offers grants and financial assistance to service members and their families who are facing financial hardship, whether due to an emergency, unexpected medical costs, or PCS-related expenses. By connecting with AFRT, you can access resources and relief when life throws curveballs your way.

Exercise: Make a List of Available Discounts and Benefits to Start Using Immediately

Now it's time to get proactive! Start by identifying which discounts and benefits you and your family can begin using today. By taking the first step toward maximizing the resources available to you, you'll save money and ease some of the financial pressure that comes with military life.

1. **List of Military Discounts**

    - Retail stores you regularly shop at that offer military discounts:
        - _____
        - _____
        - _____

    - Restaurants where you've received or can get a military discount:

- • _____
- • _____
- • _____

- Travel and entertainment discounts you've used or want to explore:
  - • _____
  - • _____
  - • _____

2. **Commissary and Exchange Savings**
   - Are you regularly using the commissary or exchanges? If not, plan your next trip:
     - • _____
     - • _____
     - • _____

3. **Free Financial Counseling Services**
   - Have you taken advantage of Military OneSource financial counseling?
     - • YES / NO
   - If no, schedule an appointment with a financial counselor today:
     - • _____

4. **Other Resources**

- Research any additional programs that could benefit your family:
  - _____
  - _____
  - _____

5. **Maximize Your Military Resources**
   - Are you fully utilizing your benefits and discounts? If not, make a plan to explore more resources.
     - _____
     - _____
     - _____

By taking full advantage of the discounts and resources available to military families, you're making an active choice to stretch your budget and increase your financial security. These benefits are here to help you—and now, it's time to use them!

Action Steps:
1. Review your regular shopping and dining habits, and identify discounts you can start using today.
2. Make a plan to visit your commissary or exchange to take advantage of savings on groceries and household goods.
3. Schedule an appointment with Military OneSource or another financial counseling service to get personalized advice.

4. Research additional military programs that can help you in your unique financial situation.

5. Make it a habit to ask about military discounts whenever you shop or dine out.

You have the resources to thrive, and using them strategically will make a huge impact on your financial journey. Keep looking for opportunities to save, and take full advantage of the military benefits that are yours to use!

Chapter 7
Renting vs. Buying with Frequent Moves

One of the most common financial decisions military families face is whether to rent or buy a home. With the unpredictability of military life—frequent moves, deployments, and career transitions—it can be hard to know if homeownership is a feasible option or if renting makes more sense. The good news is, you're not alone in making this decision, and there are strategies and resources to help guide you.

In this chapter, we'll explore the pros and cons of homeownership versus renting in the context of military life. We'll also dive into the powerful tool that is the VA loan—one of the most valuable benefits available to service members and their families. Understanding how to use this benefit to your advantage can help you make the best financial decision for your future.

Let's break down these options so you can make an informed decision about what's best for you and your family.

Evaluating the Pros and Cons of Homeownership for Military Families

Homeownership is often seen as the ultimate goal in personal finance, and while it can be a great way to build long-term wealth, it's not always the best option for military families. The decision depends on where you are in your military career, how long you plan to stay at your current duty station, and your family's financial goals. Here's a look at both sides of the equation:

- **Pros of Homeownership:**
    - **Building Equity:** With each mortgage payment, you're building equity in your home, rather than paying rent to someone else. Over time, this can contribute to long-term wealth creation.
    - **Stability and Control:** Owning a home gives you more control over your living space. You can renovate or personalize it to suit your needs, and you don't have to worry about a landlord raising rent or deciding to sell.
    - **Tax Benefits:** Homeowners may be able to take advantage of tax deductions, such as

deducting mortgage interest and property taxes.
- **Use of VA Loan:** If you qualify, you can access a VA loan, which makes homeownership more accessible, especially if you're struggling with a down payment.
- **Cons of Homeownership:**
  - **Frequent Moves:** Military families can be relocated frequently, sometimes before your home's value has had time to appreciate significantly. This can result in selling your home at a loss or dealing with the stress of managing a property from afar.
  - **Maintenance and Expenses:** Owning a home means you're responsible for maintenance, repairs, and unexpected expenses. If you're always moving, this can become burdensome.
  - **Potential Financial Risk:** If the housing market takes a downturn or if you're forced to sell quickly, you may end up with less than you paid for the house, which can impact your finances.

Using VA Loans: Advantages, Limitations, and How to Qualify

One of the most valuable benefits for military families is the **VA loan**. The VA loan is a government-backed mortgage designed to help service members, veterans, and their families purchase homes with favorable terms. If you qualify, the VA loan can make homeownership a more realistic and affordable option, especially when you consider the military lifestyle's frequent moves.

- **Advantages of VA Loans:**
    - **No Down Payment:** One of the biggest advantages of a VA loan is that it requires **no down payment** in most cases. This means you don't need to save up thousands of dollars before buying your home, which can be a significant hurdle for many families.
    - **No Private Mortgage Insurance (PMI):** Unlike conventional loans that often require PMI if your down payment is less than 20%, the VA loan does not require PMI. This can save you hundreds of dollars each month.
    - **Lower Interest Rates:** VA loans typically come with **lower interest rates** compared to conventional loans, which means lower monthly payments over the life of the loan.
    - **Flexible Qualification Requirements:** The VA loan tends to have more lenient

qualification requirements when compared to conventional loans, especially if you have a less-than-perfect credit score or a more irregular income stream.
- **Limitations of VA Loans:**
  - **Primary Residence Requirement:** A VA loan is intended for purchasing a primary residence. You cannot use it to buy a second home or investment property.
  - **Funding Fee:** While the VA loan does not require a down payment, it does come with a funding fee, which helps cover the costs of the program. However, this fee can be rolled into the loan itself, so you don't have to pay it upfront.
  - **Eligibility:** To qualify for a VA loan, you must meet certain service requirements, such as length of service or whether you were discharged under conditions other than dishonorable.
  - **Appraisal and Inspection:** The VA requires a property appraisal and inspection to ensure that the home meets certain standards. This may be more stringent than the requirements for conventional loans.

Exercise: Assess Whether Renting or Buying Is Right for Your Family

Now that you have a better understanding of the pros and cons of both renting and buying, it's time to assess which option is right for your family. Remember, this decision should be based on your specific circumstances, such as how long you plan to stay in one location, your financial goals, and the current state of the housing market. Take some time to reflect on the following:

1. **How long do you expect to stay at your current duty station?**
    - Less than 1 year: Renting may be the better choice to avoid the costs of buying and selling.
    - 1-3 years: If the housing market is favorable and you qualify for a VA loan, buying may make sense.
    - More than 3 years: Homeownership could be a good option, especially if you plan to settle in the area for an extended period.
2. **What is your financial situation?**
    - Do you have enough savings for a down payment or can you take advantage of a VA loan?
    - Are you prepared for the costs of home maintenance, taxes, and insurance?
3. **What is the housing market like in your current area?**

- Is the housing market stable, or are prices expected to rise or fall significantly in the near future?
- Will you be able to sell the home if you're relocated in the next few years, or is it better to rent?

4. **How mobile is your family?**
    - Will the nature of your military career require you to move frequently? If so, renting might be a more flexible and lower-risk option.

Your Decision

After reflecting on these questions, make a decision that fits your family's current situation and long-term goals. If you decide that buying is right for you, take full advantage of the VA loan program and other military benefits to make the process easier and more affordable. If renting makes more sense for now, that's okay too—flexibility is one of the biggest advantages of military life!

Action Steps:

1. Review your current situation and determine how long you plan to stay at your current duty station.
2. If you're considering buying, research the VA loan eligibility requirements and the current housing market in your area.

3. Compare the costs and benefits of renting versus buying, including long-term financial implications.

4. Make a plan for either renting or buying that fits your family's financial goals and military lifestyle.

Whatever you choose, remember that the goal is to make a decision that supports your family's financial well-being and gives you the flexibility to adapt to future military moves. Homeownership may be a great opportunity, but it's important to balance that with your mobility, savings, and long-term plans. You've got this!

Chapter 8
PCS (Permanent Change of Station) Planning

One of the most significant challenges military families face is the Permanent Change of Station (PCS) move. With frequent relocations and the whirlwind of adjusting to a new duty station, it's easy for your finances to take a hit. However, with a little planning, you can minimize the financial disruption and make your PCS move a smooth transition.

In this chapter, we'll break down the financial aspects of PCS planning. We'll cover budgeting for moving expenses, tracking reimbursements, and how to avoid common financial pitfalls that can arise during a relocation. By being proactive, you can maintain financial stability even in the midst of change. Plus, we'll walk you through creating a PCS financial checklist that will help you stay on top of all the moving pieces.

Let's dive into the steps that will empower you to make your next PCS move less stressful and more financially manageable.

Financial Tips for Smooth PCS Transitions

PCS moves can be both exciting and stressful, but with the right financial mindset and strategy, you can ensure that the transition is as smooth as possible. Here are key tips to help you manage the financial aspects of your move:

- **Start Early and Plan Ahead:**
  The earlier you begin planning your PCS move, the better prepared you'll be financially. Begin by estimating the costs of the move, including transportation, temporary housing, moving services, and any new purchases needed for your new home. This will help you create a realistic budget.

- **Budget for Moving Expenses:**
  While the military covers certain moving expenses, there may be other costs you'll need to cover out-of-pocket. Some of these include:
    - **Packing and unpacking services** (if you choose not to do it yourself)
    - **Meals and lodging** during travel

- **Gas and vehicle maintenance** if you're driving
- **Storage** if you need to temporarily store your belongings

  It's essential to track all your expenses carefully, as many costs are reimbursed, but you'll need to submit the proper paperwork. Keep receipts for everything!

- **Track Reimbursements:**

  The military reimburses many PCS-related expenses, such as travel costs, temporary lodging expenses, and vehicle transportation fees. Be sure to understand what's eligible for reimbursement and keep accurate records.

  - **Use the Defense Travel System (DTS):** The military has an online system that allows you to submit and track reimbursements for PCS moves. Make sure you're familiar with this tool to ensure you don't miss any potential reimbursements.
  - **Keep track of out-of-pocket expenses:** While waiting for reimbursement, you may need to cover some costs upfront. Make sure you track every expense to ensure you get paid back.

- **Avoid Going into Debt:**

  A common pitfall during a PCS move is relying

on credit cards or loans to cover moving costs, especially if you're waiting for reimbursements. To avoid accumulating debt:

- **Plan and save ahead of time** for anticipated expenses.
- **Set up an emergency fund** to cover unexpected costs without resorting to credit.
- **Be mindful of non-essential expenses.** Just because you're moving doesn't mean you need to purchase new furniture or make large, unnecessary purchases. Stick to your plan to avoid overspending.

How to Minimize Disruption to Your Family's Finances During Relocations

PCS moves disrupt not only your family's routine but also your finances. However, if you take the right steps, you can minimize that disruption and keep your family's finances on track. Here's how:

- **Update Your Budget:**
  Moving can bring about unexpected expenses, so it's essential to adjust your budget for the transition. Consider how the move will affect your housing costs, transportation, utilities, and new school or daycare expenses.

- Review and update your **monthly budget** to reflect new living circumstances. For example, you may need to account for higher rent or a larger grocery bill depending on your new location.
- **Maintain a Strong Savings Cushion:** Having a solid emergency fund is crucial when dealing with the unpredictable nature of a PCS move. Having savings will allow you to manage any unforeseen costs without derailing your financial plan.
  - Aim to keep **3-6 months of living expenses** set aside in your emergency fund to cover unexpected moving costs, delays, or other emergencies. This will give you peace of mind during your transition.
- **Avoid Interruptions to Income:** Many military families experience a temporary gap in income between moves. If you or your spouse works in the civilian sector, be sure to plan for this period of unemployment, or consider starting the job search before the move.
  - For service members, ensure you're familiar with the timeline for your paychecks during a PCS move. Some moves may cause a delay in your pay, so

having a buffer in your savings will prevent financial stress.

- **Keep Credit Accounts Organized:**
  If you have credit cards or loans, ensure that your payments are set up to continue uninterrupted during your move. Consider setting up automatic payments or extending payment due dates if necessary to avoid late fees.

  - Make sure your **address and contact information** are updated with banks, credit card companies, and loan servicers so that there are no issues with billing or payments during your move.

Exercise: Create a PCS Financial Checklist for Your Next Move

Now that you have a better understanding of how to manage the financial aspects of a PCS move, it's time to create a PCS financial checklist. This will help ensure you stay organized and on top of every detail during the process.

1. **Before the Move:**
   - Estimate moving expenses (travel, lodging, packing, etc.)
   - Set a PCS budget and create a financial cushion.

- Research reimbursement options and track eligible expenses.
- Review your moving benefits through the military and ensure you're using them.
- Start saving for any out-of-pocket expenses (packing services, food, gas, etc.).
- Update your address and contact info with all necessary institutions (banks, insurance, etc.).

2. **During the Move:**

    - Track all moving-related expenses, including receipts for meals, lodging, and travel.
    - Submit reimbursements as soon as possible.
    - Stay within your budget, and avoid unnecessary purchases during the transition.
    - Keep records of any issues with delayed reimbursements or unforeseen expenses.

3. **After the Move:**

    - Update your budget to reflect new housing, utilities, and other living expenses.
    - Begin searching for local job opportunities if applicable.
    - Keep a close eye on any outstanding reimbursements or payments.

- Re-establish your savings goals and emergency fund in your new location.

By following this checklist, you'll ensure that your finances stay organized and under control during the PCS transition, allowing you to focus more on settling in and less on financial stress.

Action Steps:

1. Create your PCS financial checklist based on the suggestions above.
2. Estimate and track all moving-related expenses.
3. Research reimbursement options and start planning for upcoming costs.
4. Make sure your budget is updated to reflect the new costs of living in your new duty station.

A PCS move doesn't have to be financially overwhelming. With proper planning, tracking, and a proactive mindset, you can reduce the stress and stay on top of your financial goals. Every move is a new opportunity to build financial strength, and with these steps, you'll be ready for success!

Chapter 9

Protecting Your Assets During Deployments

Deployments are a part of military life, but they don't have to leave your finances or assets vulnerable. As a military family, you're faced with the challenge of protecting your home, car, and belongings while being thousands of miles away. It's crucial to have a strategy in place to safeguard everything that matters to you during your time away.

In this chapter, we'll discuss essential steps to protect your financial assets while deployed. We'll explore how to secure your home and car, set up a financial power of attorney to manage money seamlessly, and take steps to ensure that all your assets are well-managed in your absence. With a little preparation, you can leave for deployment knowing that your financial future is in good hands.

Safeguarding Your Home, Car, and Belongings While Away

Your home, car, and personal belongings are often your most valuable assets. When you deploy, you want to make sure everything stays safe and protected. Here's how to ensure your assets are well taken care of while you're gone:

- **Home Protection:**
    - **Rent or Secure Your Home:** If you're renting, make sure your lease is covered during your absence. Consider negotiating a sublease or asking a trusted friend or family member to help with any issues. If you're a homeowner, ensure your mortgage payments are set up on autopay so they aren't missed while you're away.
    - **Home Insurance:** Check your home insurance policy to ensure it covers theft, damage, or natural disasters. Some policies might need to be updated based on your deployment location. Also, if you're leaving your home vacant for an extended period, notify your insurance company, as some policies have restrictions on coverage if the property is unoccupied for too long.
    - **Security Measures:** If you're not renting or living on base, consider installing a security system or surveillance cameras. A smart security system can provide peace of mind,

allowing you to monitor your property remotely. Ensure that someone reliable is checking on your home occasionally if needed.

- **Car Protection:**
    - **Vehicle Maintenance:** Before deployment, make sure your car is in good working condition. Take care of any repairs, oil changes, and maintenance. If you're leaving the car behind, it may be worth storing it in a secure location or with a trusted friend or family member.
    - **Car Insurance:** Confirm that your auto insurance will cover any potential damages or theft while you're gone. In some cases, you might qualify for a lower premium while your vehicle is in storage or not being used. Don't forget to verify that your policy covers damages outside your usual area (especially if you're leaving for a location overseas).
    - **Temporary Storage Options:** If you plan on leaving your car parked for an extended time, you might want to consider renting a storage unit for added protection. A secure garage or storage facility will shield your car from weather and theft.

- **Personal Belongings and Valuable Items:**
    - **Inventory Your Valuables:** Take an inventory of your valuables—whether it's jewelry, electronics, or important documents—and store them in a safe, secure place. This could be a fireproof safe at home or a safety deposit box at a bank.
    - **Special Considerations for High-Value Items:** For items like collectibles, artwork, or heirlooms, consider asking your insurance company if you need to get additional coverage to protect against theft or damage while you're deployed.

Setting Up Financial Power of Attorney for Seamless Money Management

Deployments can make it difficult to manage day-to-day finances, but with the right tools, you can ensure your financial matters are handled smoothly while you're away. One of the best ways to do this is by setting up a financial power of attorney (POA).

A **financial power of attorney** is a legal document that grants someone you trust the authority to manage your finances on your behalf. This can be essential for making sure bills are paid, investments are managed, and important financial decisions are made in your absence.

Here's how to set up a financial power of attorney:

- **Choose a Trusted Person:** Select someone you trust completely to manage your finances—this might be your spouse, a close relative, or a close friend. Ensure that they are organized and financially responsible, as they'll be handling significant matters in your absence.

- **Define Powers Clearly:** Be specific about what powers you're granting them. You may only need them to handle routine matters, such as paying bills, filing taxes, or managing investments. On the other hand, you may need them to handle more complex tasks like selling property or accessing bank accounts.

- **Create the Document:** You can typically draft a financial POA through your legal office on base or a local lawyer. The document should specify the powers granted, the time frame, and any limits on authority. Some military legal offices offer free assistance with setting up a POA for deployed service members.

- **Ensure Accessibility:** Once you've set up the POA, give the trusted person access to all the necessary accounts and information. Ensure they know how to access important financial records, your bills, and any other details they need to manage your finances efficiently.

- **Review Regularly:** If you set up a POA, review it regularly to make sure it aligns with your current financial situation and your deployment. If any changes are necessary, update the document to ensure your assets remain protected.

Exercise: List All Accounts, Policies, and Assets to Ensure They're Properly Managed During Deployments

Now that you have an understanding of the steps to protect your assets, it's time to ensure you're fully prepared. Use the following exercise to create a comprehensive list of your accounts, policies, and assets, so you can ensure they're all properly managed while you're deployed.

1. **Create a List of Accounts:**
   - Bank accounts (checking, savings, and investment accounts)
   - Credit card accounts
   - Retirement accounts (TSP, IRAs, pensions)
   - Loan accounts (car loans, personal loans, mortgages)
2. **Insurance Policies:**
   - Homeowners/renters insurance

- Auto insurance
- Life insurance
- Health insurance
- Other valuable items (personal property, collectibles, etc.)

3. **Assets:**
   - Homes (current, rental properties, etc.)
   - Vehicles
   - Valuable personal property (jewelry, electronics, etc.)
   - Business assets (if applicable)

4. **Power of Attorney:**
   - List the person(s) you've designated as your power of attorney.
   - Specify the powers granted and any limitations.
   - Provide them with access to all the necessary accounts and records.

5. **Emergency Contacts:**
   - List anyone who should be contacted in case of an emergency related to your finances or assets.

By completing this exercise, you'll have a clear overview of everything that needs to be managed while you're deployed, and you'll ensure that all your important assets are well-protected.

Action Steps:

1. Create your list of accounts, policies, and assets as described above.
2. Set up or update your financial power of attorney to ensure seamless financial management.
3. Review your insurance policies to make sure they cover all your assets during your deployment.
4. Make sure your designated POA person has all the necessary information to manage your finances effectively.

Deployment doesn't have to mean financial chaos. With careful planning, you can protect your home, car, and other valuable assets, ensuring that everything is managed smoothly while you're away. By taking these steps, you'll have peace of mind, knowing that your finances are in good hands—whether you're on deployment or at home.

Chapter 10
Retirement Planning with the TSP

As a member of the military, your retirement is just as important as your career advancement. And one of the best tools available to you is the **Thrift Savings Plan (TSP)**. Whether you're just starting your military career or approaching retirement, the TSP can be a game-changer in ensuring that you have the financial security you need for life after service.

In this chapter, we'll dive into how to maximize your contributions to the TSP, explain the **Blended Retirement System (BRS)** and how it affects your retirement benefits, and provide you with an actionable exercise to help you set and achieve your retirement savings goals. This chapter is designed to help you take control of your future and build the retirement you've always dreamed of.

Maximizing Your Contributions to the Thrift Savings Plan (TSP)

The **TSP** is a powerful retirement savings tool for military members. It offers low-cost investment options, tax advantages, and the ability to save consistently for the future. But how do you make the most of it?

Here's how to maximize your contributions to the TSP:

- **Contribute the Maximum Amount:**
  The TSP allows you to contribute up to a certain percentage of your income each year. In 2024, the limit for annual contributions is $22,500 (or $30,000 if you're over 50 and taking advantage of catch-up contributions). Aiming to contribute the maximum each year can significantly grow your retirement savings over time.

- **Take Full Advantage of Matching Contributions:**
  If you're part of the **Blended Retirement System (BRS)**, the government will match your contributions up to a certain percentage. For every dollar you contribute to your TSP, the government will match 1% of your base pay automatically, and you can receive up to 5% in matching contributions if you contribute at least that amount. Don't leave free money on the table—be sure to contribute at least 5% to maximize this benefit!

- **Diversify Your Investments:**
The TSP offers a variety of investment options, ranging from government bonds to stock funds. You can choose to invest in **G Fund** (Government Securities), **C Fund** (Common Stocks), **S Fund** (Small-Cap Stocks), and others, depending on your risk tolerance and retirement timeline. A diversified portfolio helps spread risk while offering the potential for greater returns over the long term.
    - **C Fund** (stocks) offers high growth potential but with more risk.
    - **G Fund** (bonds) provides stability with lower risk but less growth potential.
    - **F Fund** (bonds) focuses on corporate and government bonds.
    - **S Fund** (small-cap stocks) targets smaller companies, offering high growth potential with risk.

    Balancing these funds according to your goals and risk tolerance is essential for building a retirement portfolio that works for you.

- **Take Advantage of Automatic Contributions:**
The beauty of the TSP is that it's easy to set up automatic deductions from your paycheck. This ensures you're contributing regularly without

having to think about it. Setting up an automatic contribution plan, and making adjustments as your income grows, is a key strategy for consistent retirement savings.

Understanding the Blended Retirement System (BRS)

The **Blended Retirement System (BRS)** is the retirement system for service members who joined the military after January 1, 2018. BRS combines a traditional pension with the Thrift Savings Plan (TSP), giving you the best of both worlds: a steady income stream upon retirement and a way to build your own retirement savings through TSP contributions.

Here's what you need to know about BRS:

- **The Pension Component (Defined Benefit):** Under BRS, you will receive a pension after serving at least 20 years. The pension is calculated based on your years of service and your average base pay. The benefit starts at 40% of your average base pay after 20 years of service and increases by an additional 2.5% for each year beyond 20 years of service. The longer you serve, the larger your pension.

- **The TSP Component (Defined Contribution):** In addition to the pension, you'll receive contributions to your TSP. The government automatically contributes 1% of your base pay to your TSP as soon as you start serving, and you can contribute more (up to 5% for the government to match your contributions dollar-for-dollar). This component allows you to build your own nest egg, which can be accessed upon retirement or later in life.

- **The Lump-Sum Option:**
  If you retire before 20 years, you can still receive your TSP contributions and the government's matching contributions, but you won't be eligible for the pension. However, you can opt to receive a lump-sum payment for your TSP and pension if you're eligible. This option can give you flexibility and more control over your savings if you decide to retire early.

Understanding how BRS works will help you make more informed decisions about how much to contribute to your TSP and how to plan for your retirement. It's crucial to consider how BRS fits into your overall financial plan, especially as you plan for retirement outside of the military.

Exercise: Set a Retirement Savings Goal and Review Your Current TSP Allocations

Now that you know how to maximize your TSP contributions and understand the benefits of the Blended Retirement System, it's time to put this knowledge into action. In this exercise, you'll set a retirement savings goal and review your current TSP allocations.

1. **Set a Retirement Savings Goal:**
    - **Short-Term Goal:** Decide how much you want to contribute to your TSP over the next year. This could be a percentage of your monthly income or a fixed dollar amount.
    - **Long-Term Goal:** Consider how much you want in your TSP by the time you retire. A good starting point is to aim for 10-15% of your annual salary to be saved in the TSP each year. Remember, the earlier you start contributing, the more time your money has to grow.
2. **Review Your Current TSP Allocations:**
    - Log into your TSP account and review your current contributions and fund allocations.
    - Are you contributing enough to take full advantage of the government's matching contributions? If not, consider adjusting your contributions to at least 5%.

- Are your investments aligned with your risk tolerance and long-term goals? Consider diversifying your portfolio by including a mix of different TSP funds to balance risk and return.
- If you're not sure about the best way to allocate your TSP funds, consider consulting a financial advisor or using one of the TSP's default allocation options (like the Lifecycle Funds).

3. **Action Steps:**

   - Increase your contributions if you're not yet at 5% to take full advantage of the government's match.
   - Make sure your TSP allocations are diversified based on your financial goals and timeline.
   - Review and adjust your goals annually to stay on track for a comfortable retirement.

Action Steps:

1. Set your retirement savings goal for both the short and long term.
2. Log into your TSP account and ensure your current contributions and allocations align with your goals.
3. Increase your contributions to at least 5% to receive the full government match.

4. Review and adjust your retirement plan regularly to ensure you're on track.

Retirement planning isn't something to put off for later—it's something you can start today. By maximizing your TSP contributions and understanding how the Blended Retirement System works, you're already taking important steps toward a secure and fulfilling retirement. Keep pushing forward, stay disciplined, and trust that your efforts now will pay off when you retire from military service. Your future self will thank you!

Chapter 11
Investing for Military Families

As a military family, your life is filled with change—frequent moves, deployments, and career transitions. But one thing that can bring stability to your financial future is **investing**. It's an empowering way to grow your wealth, even with the unpredictable nature of military life. Whether you're just starting to invest or looking to refine your strategy, this chapter is all about how to start small, stay flexible, and balance your investment options to secure your future.

You don't need to have a massive salary or years of investing experience to get started. In fact, some of the best investors started with just a little bit, staying consistent, and investing over time. This chapter will guide you through how to begin investing, even on a tight budget, and how to manage your investments while navigating the unique challenges of military life.

Starting with Small Investments While Managing a Mobile Lifestyle

One of the most common concerns for military families is how to invest while managing the challenges of a **mobile lifestyle**. Frequent moves, deployments, and the need for flexibility can make long-term investing seem complicated. But the reality is that it's not only possible—it's essential.

Here's how to get started:

- **Start Small and Consistent:**
  You don't need a large sum of money to begin investing. Small, consistent contributions can grow over time, especially if you're investing in tax-advantaged accounts like the **Thrift Savings Plan (TSP)** or a **Roth IRA**. Think of it like planting a tree: the earlier you start, the more time it has to grow. Even if you can only afford to invest $50 a month, start there and increase it as your finances allow.

- **Focus on Low-Cost, Flexible Investments:**
  As a military family, you might not have the time or resources to research and manage individual stocks, but that doesn't mean you can't invest. **Index funds** and **ETFs (Exchange-Traded Funds)** offer a great way to invest in a broad range of stocks or bonds without the need for

active management. These investments tend to be low-cost and provide broad diversification, which is a key strategy for reducing risk. This is important because, with the unpredictability of military life, you need to ensure your investments are working for you without requiring constant attention.

- **Leverage Automatic Contributions:**
The same way you set up automatic contributions to your **TSP**, you can do the same for other investment accounts. By setting up automatic withdrawals from your bank account or paycheck to invest in an IRA or taxable brokerage account, you ensure that investing becomes a habit. Automation allows you to "pay yourself first" without thinking about it, and consistency is key to building wealth over time.

- **Consider Investing in Target-Date Funds:**
If you're uncertain about how to allocate your investments or how to balance your risk tolerance, **target-date funds** are a great option. These funds automatically adjust the asset allocation (stocks, bonds, etc.) based on your retirement target year. For example, if you plan to retire in 30 years, the fund will be more heavily invested in stocks, which typically offer higher returns but come with more risk. As you get closer to retirement, the

fund will shift towards more stable investments like bonds.

Balancing Retirement Accounts, Taxable Investments, and Education Savings Plans

It's easy to get caught up in retirement savings and forget about other essential investments, like those for **your children's education** or taxable investment accounts that can provide more flexibility. But balancing all these different accounts will help you create a well-rounded financial plan.

Here's a breakdown of how to think about these accounts:

- **Retirement Accounts (TSP, IRAs, Roth IRAs):** These accounts are your long-term wealth-building tools. **TSP** is your military retirement account, but don't overlook the power of an **IRA** (Individual Retirement Account). Both **Traditional IRAs** and **Roth IRAs** offer tax advantages. With a **Traditional IRA**, you contribute pre-tax dollars, reducing your taxable income for the year. However, when you withdraw funds in retirement, they are taxed. With a **Roth IRA**, you contribute after-tax dollars, but your investments grow tax-free, and you can withdraw them tax-free in retirement. The key is to contribute to these accounts regularly and maximize your contributions whenever possible. Consider using a **Roth IRA** if you're early in your career and in a lower tax bracket, so you can benefit from tax-free growth.

- **Taxable Investment Accounts:**
  While retirement accounts are essential for long-term savings, taxable investment accounts provide flexibility. Unlike retirement accounts, you can access the funds in a taxable account without penalty before retirement age. This flexibility is key, especially when your military career might have periods of transition. In these accounts, you can invest in individual stocks, bonds, or ETFs, and you'll be taxed on the gains and dividends when you sell. It's a great way to invest extra funds while maintaining flexibility.

- **Education Savings Plans (529 Plans):**
  If you're planning to save for your children's education, a **529 College Savings Plan** is a great option. This account allows you to invest after-tax dollars and then withdraw the money tax-free for qualified education expenses. Many states even offer a state tax deduction for contributions to a 529 plan. If you're moving often, many 529 plans are portable across state lines, so you can take them with you no matter where you're stationed.

Exercise: Open an Investment Account or Review Your Portfolio for Diversification

Now that you have a better understanding of the different investment options available, it's time to take action. Here's a simple exercise to get you started:

1. **Open an Investment Account:**
    - If you haven't already, open a **Roth IRA** or **Traditional IRA** with a brokerage firm. Many firms, like Vanguard, Fidelity, and Charles Schwab, offer no-fee IRAs. You can start with a low minimum investment, and the process is straightforward.
    - Consider opening a **taxable brokerage account** to begin investing outside of retirement accounts, if you have extra funds you want to put to work for you.
2. **Review Your Current Portfolio:**
    - If you already have an investment account, take time to review your **asset allocation**. Are you diversified enough? If your portfolio is overly concentrated in one sector, such as technology, consider rebalancing it. A diversified portfolio—spread across different types of assets (stocks, bonds, real estate, etc.)—helps

protect your wealth from the volatility of any one market sector.
- If you're investing through a **TSP**, check if you're contributing enough to get the full government match. Review your current investment allocation to ensure it matches your long-term goals. If you're closer to retirement, consider moving some of your funds into more conservative options like the **G Fund**.

3. **Set Investment Goals:**

- Set specific goals for your investments. Are you saving for retirement, your child's education, or a down payment on a home? Write down how much you need to contribute each month to reach those goals. Track your progress and adjust your contributions as your situation changes.

4. **Take Action:**

- Set up an automatic contribution plan for your **TSP**, IRA, and taxable investment accounts. Automating your contributions will help you stay consistent in building wealth.
- Start small if you need to, but take the first step to make your money work for you.

Action Steps:
1. Open an IRA or taxable brokerage account if you don't already have one.
2. Review your current investment portfolio for diversification and balance.
3. Set specific investment goals for retirement, education savings, or other financial priorities.
4. Set up automatic contributions to stay consistent and grow your wealth over time.

Conclusion: Investing doesn't have to be intimidating or complicated. By starting small, staying consistent, and leveraging the power of automation, you can build wealth over time, even as you navigate the unique challenges of military life. Whether you're investing for retirement, education, or other goals, the key is to start today and stay committed to your financial future.

In the next chapter, we'll dive deeper into how to plan for a financially secure future, even when you're juggling the demands of deployments, moves, and everything else military life throws your way. Keep up the momentum—you're building a strong financial foundation for your family, and that's something to be proud of!

Chapter 12
Building Passive Income Streams

Military life offers a unique set of challenges, but it also presents countless opportunities to build wealth and secure your financial future. One of the smartest ways to achieve financial freedom is through **passive income**—money that comes in regularly without requiring constant effort on your part. Whether you're looking for a side hustle or want to invest in assets that work for you, passive income can be a game-changer.

Building passive income allows you to diversify your financial portfolio and create more flexibility, especially in the unpredictable world of military life. The beauty of passive income is that it doesn't require your full-time attention, making it a perfect fit for the military lifestyle, where moves and deployments often disrupt traditional employment. In this chapter, we'll explore how military families can tap into side hustles and investment opportunities that create long-term financial stability.

Side Hustles that Work for Military Families

Starting a side hustle doesn't mean giving up your full-time commitment to the military or your family. It's about creating extra streams of income that fit seamlessly into your schedule and goals. The key to success is choosing hustles that are flexible, scalable, and manageable during deployments or frequent moves.

Here are some ideas for **side hustles** that can work for military families:

- **Online Businesses:**
    - Starting an online business is one of the most flexible ways to generate passive income. Whether it's an **e-commerce store**, **digital products**, or offering **freelance services**, the online world provides a wealth of opportunities.
    - Consider starting an **affiliate marketing** website, where you promote other people's products and earn a commission for each sale made through your referral link. You can also create and sell **digital products** like eBooks, online courses, or design templates, which require minimal ongoing effort once created.

- **Blogging or YouTube:**
    - Sharing your experiences, whether through a **military family blog** or a **YouTube channel**, can eventually turn into a lucrative passive income stream. Over time, once you've built an audience, you can monetize through **ads**, **sponsorships**, and **affiliate links**.
    - Blogs and YouTube channels can focus on a variety of topics—**military life**, **finance**, **parenting**, **fitness**, or **DIY projects**. If you're consistent and authentic, you can grow a loyal following and create a business that generates passive income.
- **Real Estate Investments:**
    - Real estate is one of the most tried-and-true ways to create passive income. As a military family, you may have the advantage of moving to different areas and potentially securing good deals on rental properties. If you're strategic, you can build a portfolio of rental properties that generate consistent monthly cash flow.
    - Consider investing in **single-family homes**, **multi-family units**, or even **vacation rentals**. Platforms like **Airbnb** can offer a flexible rental option, especially if you're

stationed in an area that attracts tourists or travelers.

- **Remote Work Opportunities:**
  - With remote work becoming more common, you can leverage your military experience and skills for remote jobs that offer flexible hours. Whether it's **virtual assistance**, **social media management**, **consulting**, or **freelance writing**, the possibilities are endless. These jobs allow you to work from anywhere, meaning you can still have a steady income stream without being tied to one location.

Leveraging Military Housing Benefits for Rental Property Investments

One of the most significant financial advantages for military families is the **Basic Allowance for Housing (BAH)**. This allowance can be used for rent, utilities, and other housing expenses, but what many military families don't realize is that **BAH can also be leveraged for investment purposes**.

If you're stationed in a location with a high BAH rate, you may be able to use the extra funds to invest in rental properties. Here's how you can start using military housing benefits to build wealth:

- **Buy a Home with BAH:**
If you've been at your duty station for a while or are planning to stay for a few years, buying a home might be a smart investment. With the help of the **VA loan**, you can purchase a home with little to no down payment and relatively low interest rates. The key is to find a home that's under the BAH amount to keep your monthly payments low.

- **Rent Out Part of Your Property:**
If you buy a home, consider renting out part of it, such as an extra room or a separate apartment in a multi-unit property. This rental income can cover your mortgage or even become a profitable passive income stream.

- **Consider VA Loans for Investment Properties:**
While VA loans are typically used for primary residences, you can buy a property with a VA loan and later rent it out once you PCS. As long as you're moving to a new duty station and your previous property is no longer your primary residence, you can rent out the home and use the rental income to cover your new housing expenses.

- **Explore House Hacking:**
House hacking is a popular real estate investment

strategy where you buy a property and rent out rooms or units to others. This allows you to reduce your own living expenses while building equity in your property. Military families can often make this strategy work, particularly when stationed in high-demand areas.

Exercise: Brainstorm One Passive Income Stream You Can Start Building

Now that you understand the power of passive income and how it can work for you, it's time to take action. Choose one passive income stream to start building, even if it's just a small step toward something bigger. Here's how to brainstorm and plan your next steps:

1. **Consider Your Strengths and Interests:**
    - What are you passionate about? What skills do you already have that could translate into a profitable side hustle or investment? Whether you're a DIY enthusiast, a writer, a techie, or someone who loves to teach, there are plenty of ways to turn your passions into income.
2. **Look for Opportunities in Your Current Situation:**
    - How can you use your military life to your advantage? Are there places you're

stationed that have a strong rental market? Could you start a blog or YouTube channel documenting your experiences? Can you leverage your BAH for real estate investments? Reflect on how you can take what you already have and turn it into passive income.

3. **Start Small and Stay Consistent:**

    - You don't have to go big right away. Start with a small project, like creating a simple blog or investing in a single rental property. Focus on consistency and gradual growth over time. Remember, even small efforts can add up to big rewards in the long run.

4. **Set Actionable Goals:**

    - Write down one passive income idea you're excited about and set a goal to take the first step. Whether that's researching real estate investment, signing up for an online course, or setting up an account to start an e-commerce business, take action today.

Action Steps:

1. Brainstorm a passive income idea based on your interests and military lifestyle.
2. Set a specific goal and timeline to take the first step.

3. Research ways to leverage military benefits for real estate or other income streams.
4. Start small and stay consistent—passive income takes time to grow!

Conclusion: Building passive income is one of the smartest financial strategies you can use to achieve financial independence. Whether you're investing in real estate, starting an online business, or using your military benefits creatively, the key is to start today and stay committed. Even if you're only able to invest a little time or money right now, you're laying the foundation for a more financially secure and flexible future.

In the next chapter, we'll discuss how to **stay motivated** as you work towards your financial goals, even in the face of military life's uncertainties. Keep building, keep striving, and remember—your financial future is in your hands!

Chapter 13
Transitioning to Civilian Life

The day will come when your military service ends, whether you've chosen to retire or are transitioning to civilian life after your contract ends. It's a significant milestone, and while it may bring about new challenges, it's also an incredible opportunity to take control of your future and make your financial dreams a reality. The key to a successful transition is **planning**—financially, personally, and professionally.

Transitioning from military service can be a complex process, but with the right strategies and mindset, you can thrive in civilian life just as you did in the military. The skills you've developed during your service—discipline, leadership, teamwork, and perseverance—will continue to serve you well as you navigate your new career and financial future.

In this chapter, we'll explore how to **plan financially** for your transition, **leverage military experience** to secure high-paying civilian jobs, and create a roadmap for success once you've left active duty. By taking proactive steps, you can build a solid foundation for your post-military life and ensure that your financial goals remain on track.

Financial Planning for Retirement or Separation from the Military

Whether you're transitioning after 20 years of service or leaving after a shorter period, **financial planning** is essential. The military offers unique benefits, but as you transition, it's crucial to ensure that your financial situation is set up for success.

Here are key areas to focus on:

- **Maximize Retirement Benefits:**
  If you're retiring after 20 or more years of service, you may be eligible for military retirement benefits. However, retirement pay alone may not be enough to meet all your financial needs. It's essential to supplement your military pension with other retirement savings, such as contributions to the **Thrift Savings Plan (TSP)** or personal retirement accounts. Ensure that you have a comprehensive retirement plan that includes multiple income sources, such as savings, investments, and possibly part-time work.

- **Severance Pay and Transition Assistance:**
  If you're transitioning without retirement pay, you may receive **severance pay** based on your years of service. You'll also have access to the **Transition Assistance Program (TAP)**, which provides valuable resources, including resume-building workshops, job placement assistance, and financial planning counseling. Take full advantage of these resources to ease your transition.

- **Health Insurance:**
  One of the most significant changes when leaving the military is health care coverage. You'll likely lose eligibility for TRICARE, so plan ahead for civilian health insurance options. Research healthcare plans available through your new employer, or explore options through the **Affordable Care Act** if you're not immediately employed after transition.

- **Emergency Fund:**
  Whether you're retiring or separating, having an **emergency fund** is crucial during your transition. If you don't yet have a robust emergency fund, now is the time to build it up. An emergency fund provides a cushion for unexpected expenses and gives you peace of mind as you adjust to civilian life.

Translating Military Skills into High-Paying Civilian Careers

The skills you've acquired in the military—leadership, problem-solving, communication, and technical expertise—are highly valued in the civilian workforce. As you transition, your military experience can give you a significant edge in securing high-paying jobs, but it's important to **translate** those skills into terms that civilian employers understand.

Here are some strategies for successfully navigating the civilian job market:

- **Highlight Transferable Skills:**
  When crafting your resume, focus on the skills that are transferable to civilian careers. For example, if you've managed a team of soldiers, emphasize your leadership and project management abilities. If you've worked with complex systems, highlight your technical proficiency and problem-solving skills. Use civilian-friendly language to explain your experience, focusing on outcomes and achievements.

- **Networking:**
  Networking is crucial when transitioning to civilian employment. Attend **career fairs**, **industry events**, and **military-to-civilian**

networking groups to connect with potential employers. Leverage your military network, too—many veterans and military spouses have found success by connecting with others who understand the challenges of the transition.

- **Certifications and Education:**
  Some military members may need additional certifications or education to make a smooth transition into certain civilian industries. If you haven't already, consider pursuing certifications in areas such as **project management (PMP)**, **information technology (IT)**, or **business management**. Many military members can use their GI Bill benefits for education or certifications that will open up lucrative job opportunities.

- **Explore Civilian Jobs in Defense Contracting:**
  If you're passionate about continuing to serve in a military-related field, **defense contracting** could be an ideal option. Many companies hire veterans for their expertise in defense and security operations. Jobs in this sector often provide excellent compensation and allow you to leverage your military experience while transitioning to the civilian workforce.

Exercise: Outline a Financial Plan for Your Transition Out of Service

Now that you've explored the financial considerations of transitioning from the military, it's time to create a **detailed financial plan** for your exit from service. Whether you're retiring or separating, this exercise will help you lay the groundwork for financial success and stability.

Here's a step-by-step guide to create your financial plan:

1. **Assess Your Current Financial Situation:**
    - Review your assets, debts, income, and expenses. Take stock of your military retirement benefits (if applicable), severance pay, and savings. This will give you a clear picture of where you stand financially and help you set realistic goals for your transition.
2. **Create a Budget for Post-Military Life:**
    - Based on your expected income after leaving the military, create a **post-transition budget**. Factor in costs like civilian healthcare, housing, transportation, and any changes to your family's lifestyle. Compare your income to your projected

expenses to determine whether you'll need to make adjustments.

3. **Research Civilian Job Opportunities:**
   - Start exploring potential civilian career options and salaries. Look into industries that align with your skills and interests, and research the qualifications and certifications needed for those positions. Networking and job applications should start as early as possible to give you ample time to secure employment.

4. **Plan for Health Insurance Coverage:**
   - Research your options for civilian health insurance and factor the costs into your budget. If you'll be using the **Affordable Care Act (ACA)**, visit the marketplace to compare plans and premiums. Don't forget to explore any health coverage offered by your future employer.

5. **Build or Strengthen Your Emergency Fund:**
   - Set a goal to have **three to six months** of living expenses saved in an emergency fund. If you don't already have one, make it a priority to start saving now. This fund will help bridge the gap between military and

civilian life and provide a financial cushion in case of unexpected circumstances.

6. **Set Retirement Goals:**

   - Even if you're transitioning to civilian life, continue to prioritize your long-term retirement goals. Contribute to retirement accounts like an **IRA**, **401(k)**, or **TSP** if you're eligible. Aim to maximize your savings and ensure that you're on track to achieve financial independence in retirement.

Action Steps:

1. Review your current financial situation, including income, debts, and assets.
2. Set a budget based on your expected post-military income and expenses.
3. Explore job opportunities and certifications that will help you transition to a civilian career.
4. Research civilian health insurance options and factor them into your budget.
5. Build or strengthen your emergency fund.
6. Continue contributing to your retirement savings and set long-term financial goals.

Conclusion:

The transition from military life to civilian life is a monumental change, but with careful financial planning and strategic career moves, you can make it a smooth and successful journey. Use your military experience as a springboard for your next chapter, and stay proactive about securing your financial future.

Your military service has prepared you for greatness—now, it's time to translate that experience into civilian success. In the next chapter, we'll discuss how to **stay motivated and disciplined** as you adjust to this new phase of life. Keep pushing forward, and remember—your future is brighter than ever!

Chapter 14
Education and Career Benefits for Families

Military life isn't just about duty and sacrifice—it's also about **opportunity**. Whether you're active duty, a veteran, or a military spouse, there are incredible resources available to help you and your family invest in **education** and **career growth**. These benefits can empower you to **level up** your career, pursue educational dreams, and set your children up for future success. This chapter is all about making the most of those opportunities and ensuring your family's financial and educational future is as bright as possible.

Let's dive into some of the **key educational and career benefits** available to military families, how you can use them to your advantage, and the tools that will help you build a strong educational foundation for your family.

Using the GI Bill and MyCAA

The **GI Bill** and **MyCAA (Military Spouse Career Advancement Accounts)** are two of the most powerful resources available to military families when it comes to **higher education** and **career advancement**. These programs can provide you with the financial support needed to pursue college degrees, technical certifications, or career training.

1. **The GI Bill (Post-9/11 GI Bill)**
   The GI Bill is a game-changer for veterans and service members who want to pursue higher education. It covers tuition costs, housing allowances, and books, and it can be used for a variety of educational options, including traditional degree programs, vocational training, and even certifications. Here's how you can leverage the GI Bill:

   - **Tuition Assistance:** The GI Bill will pay for a significant portion of your tuition and fees, sometimes covering the full cost depending on the program.
   - **Housing Allowance:** If you're enrolled at least half-time, you'll be eligible for a **housing stipend** to cover your living expenses while you attend school. This is especially helpful if you're transitioning to civilian life and need financial support as you further your education.
   - **Transfer Benefits:** If you have unused GI Bill benefits, you may be able to **transfer**

them to your spouse or children, offering them the opportunity to attend college without the financial burden. This is a great way to set up your children for success and invest in their future.
2. **MyCAA (Military Spouse Career Advancement Accounts)**
For military spouses, **MyCAA** is an incredible benefit that offers up to **$4,000** in financial assistance for education and training. Whether you're interested in earning a certification in a high-demand field like healthcare, business, or information technology, MyCAA can help fund your career goals. Here's how MyCAA can benefit you:

- **Career-Focused Education:** MyCAA funds can be used for **vocational schools, certifications**, and **license programs** that are portable and can enhance your career opportunities regardless of your next PCS location.
- **Flexible Use:** Because many military spouses face challenges with frequent moves, MyCAA provides a flexible way to continue education while adapting to new circumstances.

By making the most of both the GI Bill and MyCAA, you can secure an education for yourself or your spouse that will **boost career prospects** and contribute to long-term financial success.

Saving for Your Children's Education

While the GI Bill is a fantastic resource for service members, it doesn't extend to funding your children's education. But don't worry—you can still make **smart financial moves** to ensure that your children have the opportunity to attend college without accumulating significant debt. One of the best tools for this is a **529 plan**.

1. **529 College Savings Plans**

    A **529 plan** is a tax-advantaged investment account that allows you to save for your child's college education. The beauty of a 529 plan is that the money grows tax-deferred, and withdrawals for **qualified education expenses** are tax-free. Here's why you should consider setting one up for your children:

    - **Tax Advantages:** Contributions to a 529 plan grow without being taxed, and the earnings are not taxed when withdrawn to pay for eligible educational expenses like tuition, room, board, and books.

- **Control and Flexibility:** As the account holder, you maintain control over the funds, and you can change the beneficiary if needed. If your child decides not to pursue college, you can redirect the funds to another child or even use the account for your own educational needs.
- **Portability:** A 529 plan can be used for education expenses at any accredited college, university, or technical school across the U.S. and abroad, making it a flexible choice for military families on the move.

2. **Other College Savings Options**
   While the 529 plan is a popular choice, there are other options you can explore, such as **Coverdell Education Savings Accounts (ESAs)** or **Custodial Accounts (UGMA/UTMA)**. These options have different tax implications and restrictions, but they can still be effective tools for saving for your child's education.

By setting up a college savings plan early, you're providing a solid foundation for your children's future. A little planning today can go a long way toward helping them graduate debt-free and start their own financial journey on the right foot.

Exercise: Research One Education Benefit You or Your Family Can Use

Now that you've explored the educational benefits available to military families, it's time to take action. Research one **education benefit** you or your family can take advantage of today. Here's how:

1. **For Active Duty Service Members:**
   - Check your eligibility for the **GI Bill** if you haven't already used it, or explore how to transfer it to your spouse or children.
   - Research the options available through **MyCAA** to enhance your spouse's career prospects.
2. **For Military Families with Children:**
   - Look into setting up a **529 plan** for your child's college education, or research other college savings options available to you.
3. **For Veterans and Spouses:**
   - Review the **Veteran's Education Assistance Program (VEAP)** or other state-specific benefits that can help you continue your education after military service.

Once you've selected the benefit that best fits your family's needs, take steps to get started—whether that's enrolling in a program, applying for funding, or setting up a college savings account. Don't let these powerful resources slip by—use them to fuel your family's **educational and career growth**!

Conclusion:

Military life is filled with unique challenges, but it also offers unparalleled opportunities. By taking full advantage of the **education and career benefits** available to you and your family, you're not only investing in your own future but also setting your children up for success. Whether you're pursuing higher education for yourself, advancing your spouse's career, or saving for your children's college, these benefits are a key part of your financial toolkit.

In the next chapter, we'll focus on how to **protect your family's financial future** through insurance and estate planning. Let's keep moving forward—your journey toward financial security and success is just beginning!

Chapter 15
Creating a Legacy for Future Generations

As a military family, your sacrifices and hard work don't just impact your present—they can also shape the future. **Creating a legacy** is about more than just leaving material wealth; it's about setting up your family for success and ensuring that the values, lessons, and financial wisdom you pass down will **empower future generations** to thrive.

This chapter is dedicated to helping you take steps today to **protect your family's financial future** and create a legacy of **strength**, **wisdom**, and **wealth** for your children and beyond. You have the power to make decisions today that will set the stage for a thriving, financially secure family for years to come.

Let's break down the key steps you can take to **protect your family** and **teach your children** how to build a legacy of financial success.

Protecting Your Family with Life Insurance and Estate Planning

1. **Life Insurance**
   One of the most important pieces of a **financial legacy** is ensuring that your family is **financially protected** in the event of an unexpected tragedy. Life insurance provides peace of mind, knowing that if something happens to you, your loved ones will have the financial resources they need to maintain their lifestyle and cover any unexpected costs.

   - **Term Life Insurance vs. Whole Life Insurance:**
     There are two main types of life insurance: term life and whole life. Term life insurance is typically more affordable and provides coverage for a set period (e.g., 20 or 30 years). Whole life insurance offers coverage for your entire life and includes a **cash value** component, but it's often more expensive. Both can play a role in protecting your family, so it's important to consider your **family's needs** and your **budget** when making a decision.

   - **Military Life Insurance Options:**
     The **Servicemembers' Group Life**

Insurance (SGLI) is available to active-duty military members and provides affordable life insurance coverage. It's essential to review your coverage and **adjust your policy** if needed to ensure it aligns with your family's needs, especially if your situation changes (e.g., marriage, children, home purchase).

- **Consider a Policy for Spouses:** While life insurance for service members is often a priority, it's also wise to consider coverage for your spouse, especially if they contribute to the household income. This ensures that **both incomes** are protected in the event of an unexpected loss.

2. **Estate Planning**

Estate planning is another critical component of protecting your family's future. It's not just about **wealth distribution** after you're gone; it's about ensuring that your wishes are honored, and your family is prepared for any eventuality.

- **Wills and Trusts:** A **will** is a legal document that outlines how your assets will be distributed after your death. It's essential to have a will in place, especially if you have children, to ensure that they're cared for according to your wishes. For more complex estates or to avoid the probate process, a **trust** may be beneficial. Trusts allow assets to be distributed more quickly and can provide tax advantages.

- **Power of Attorney and Healthcare Directives:**
  Powers of Attorney give someone the legal authority to make financial and legal decisions on your behalf if you become incapacitated. **Healthcare directives** provide guidance for medical care decisions if you're unable to communicate your preferences. These documents ensure that your wishes are respected in the event of illness or injury.

- **Beneficiary Designations:**
  Review your **beneficiary designations** on accounts like life insurance, retirement accounts (TSP, IRA, 401k), and any other financial accounts. Ensure they are up to date, so your assets go to the right people without complications.

Teaching Your Children Financial Literacy for Generational Wealth

Building wealth isn't just about **saving and investing**; it's also about **teaching** your children how to make sound financial decisions. Instilling a mindset of financial literacy early in their lives will help ensure they carry on the **legacy** of financial responsibility and success.

1. **Teach Them the Basics of Money Management**
   Start by teaching your children **basic financial concepts** like saving, budgeting, and investing. Help them understand the importance of **living within their means**, **setting goals**, and making informed decisions with their money. The earlier they learn these habits, the more likely they are to grow up with a healthy relationship to money.

   - **Savings:** Open a **children's savings account** or **piggy bank** and encourage them to set aside a portion of their allowance or birthday money.
   - **Budgeting:** Help them set up a simple budget, even for small amounts, to teach them how to manage their money wisely.
   - **Investing:** As they get older, introduce them to the basics of investing. Explain concepts like compound interest, stocks, and bonds in a way that makes sense for their age.

2. **Teach Them About the Power of Earning and Giving Back**
   Encourage an entrepreneurial mindset by allowing them to earn money through **part-time jobs**, **side hustles**, or starting their own business. Teach them that **wealth is built through hard work, smart decisions, and generosity**.
   - **Give to Charity:** As your children start earning, encourage them to **give back** by donating a portion of their income to causes that are important to them. This not only instills a sense of **responsibility** but also reinforces the value of **generosity** and helping others.
3. **Lead by Example**
   Children learn by watching. Demonstrate financial responsibility by modeling **good money habits** in your own life—whether that's sticking to a budget, saving for long-term goals, or investing for the future. Your actions will speak louder than words.

Exercise: Write Down Your Legacy Goals and Create an Action Plan

Now that you've learned how to protect your family and set your children up for financial success, it's time to take action. Think about the legacy you want to leave behind and the specific steps you need to take to ensure your family's financial future is secure. Here's your exercise:

1. **Write Down Your Legacy Goals**
   Reflect on the values and principles you want to pass down to your children and future generations. What financial goals do you want to achieve for your family? Some examples might include:
   - Ensuring your children have the education they need without student debt.
   - Creating a trust to pass on assets to your children.
   - Teaching your children the value of saving and investing early.

2. **Create an Action Plan**
   Break down each of your legacy goals into actionable steps. For example, if one of your goals is to **establish a college fund**, your action plan might include:
   - Opening a **529 plan** for each of your children.
   - Setting a monthly contribution goal.
   - Reviewing the plan annually to ensure you're on track.

   Keep your plan **flexible** and update it as your family's circumstances change.

Conclusion:

Creating a financial legacy is one of the most impactful gifts you can give your family. It's about **protecting** their future, teaching them essential financial skills, and setting them up for **long-term success**. By using life insurance, estate planning, and taking the time to teach your children financial literacy, you're building a foundation that will support generations to come.

In the final chapter, we'll wrap up by reviewing how everything you've learned ties together into a comprehensive financial plan for your family. Your legacy begins today—let's continue the journey of creating the future you've always dreamed of for your loved ones!

Chapter 16
Thriving Despite Challenges

Military life is full of challenges, from frequent relocations to unpredictable deployments, and the stress of balancing family needs with service obligations. Despite these uncertainties, one of the most empowering things you can do is embrace **resilience**—the ability to bounce back and keep moving forward, even when things don't go as planned.

In this chapter, we'll explore how to stay **focused on your financial goals** and **thrive**, no matter what obstacles come your way. Whether you're facing a temporary setback or a long-term disruption, your ability to **adapt, stay disciplined, and stay resilient** will ensure that you continue building the financial future you envision for yourself and your family.

Embracing Resilience in the Face of Uncertainty

Life in the military is inherently unpredictable, and at times, it can feel like **everything is up in the air**—your housing situation, your income, your deployment schedule, and your family's well-being. But resilience isn't about avoiding tough situations; it's about how you respond to them.

- **Embrace Change as Opportunity:**
  Every time you face a new challenge, it's also an opportunity for growth. Whether it's moving to a new location or adjusting to a different financial situation, view each disruption as a chance to **learn, adapt, and build new skills**. For example, a PCS (Permanent Change of Station) might mean a new set of financial hurdles, but it could also be an opportunity to find new ways to save, invest, or optimize your budget.

- **Develop Mental Toughness:**
  Resilience is as much about mindset as it is about strategy. When you face setbacks, don't see them as failures. Instead, view them as **learning experiences**. The military lifestyle teaches you to be flexible and adaptable—apply those same qualities to your finances. Remember, setbacks are not the end of the road but just a part of the journey. Stay focused on your **long-term goals**, and let short-term challenges motivate you to work even harder.

- **Stay Connected to Your Support System:**
  Resilience isn't built alone. Whether it's family,

friends, or fellow service members, make sure you lean on your support system. They're there to encourage you when you're feeling overwhelmed, offer advice when you're stuck, and remind you that you're not facing challenges alone.

Staying Focused on Long-Term Goals Despite Frequent Disruptions

Military life's **unpredictability** means that your financial plans will often face **disruptions**. Perhaps your housing allowance changes, your deployment status shifts, or a PCS throws your budget off track. These interruptions can feel like roadblocks to your goals, but they don't have to derail your progress.

Here's how you can stay on course despite the challenges:

- **Maintain a Strong "Why"**:
  The more clearly you understand why you're pursuing your financial goals, the easier it will be to stay focused, even when life gets in the way. Whether it's financial independence, a secure retirement, or building generational wealth, keep your **"why"** front and center. When the going gets tough, reminding yourself of the bigger picture will help you stay grounded.

- **Create Flexibility in Your Plan:**
Build a financial plan that is adaptable. Instead of focusing only on rigid goals, create a flexible **roadmap**. When disruptions happen, tweak your strategy rather than abandoning it altogether. If one plan isn't working due to a PCS or deployment, develop an alternative strategy. The more **flexible** your plan, the more **resilient** you'll be in the face of challenges.

- **Celebrate Small Wins:**
Even if your long-term goals seem far away, celebrate the **small victories** along the way. Whether it's paying off a credit card, saving an extra $100 this month, or hitting your savings goal, these milestones add up. Recognizing and celebrating them will **keep you motivated** and help you see that you're making progress—even if it feels slow.

Exercise: Reflect on Your Financial Wins and Areas for Growth

Now it's time for you to reflect on how you've been navigating the unpredictable nature of military life and finances. Take a moment to acknowledge your **financial wins**—the steps you've taken to manage your money well, even in the face of challenges. Then, identify areas where there's room for growth.

Here's your exercise:

1. **Financial Wins**
   Reflect on the wins you've had—big or small. These are the moments where you've overcome challenges and made progress toward your financial goals.

   - Have you built an emergency fund that has helped you through a PCS move or an unexpected expense?
   - Have you successfully navigated a deployment while maintaining control of your finances?
   - Did you maximize your TSP contributions, or start a side hustle that's now generating income?

   Write down **three financial wins** that you're proud of. Recognize the **resilience** that made them possible.

2. **Areas for Growth**
   No journey is without areas of improvement. Think about the challenges that still lie ahead. Perhaps you want to improve your investment strategy, increase your savings rate, or get better at budgeting during a PCS move.

Write down **three areas for growth**—things you'd like to improve or goals you'd like to work toward in the next year. Keep in mind that growth doesn't happen overnight. These are areas where you can **build resilience** and make incremental improvements.

3. **Action Steps**

   For each area of growth, write down a few concrete **action steps** you can take in the coming months to move forward. It might be setting up automatic savings, reviewing your TSP allocations, or learning more about investing. Make these steps **specific and achievable**.

Conclusion:

Military life is full of challenges, but your ability to **thrive despite them** will set you apart. By embracing resilience, staying focused on your long-term goals, and celebrating the small wins along the way, you'll continue building the financial future you desire. Remember, each challenge is an opportunity to grow and build the strength necessary to achieve your dreams.

In the final chapter, we'll wrap up everything you've learned and help you create a **comprehensive action plan** to continue your journey toward financial success. Keep going—you've got this!

Chapter 17
Building a Supportive Community

In the military, **community** is everything. It's a built-in support system that helps you navigate the complexities of service life, and when it comes to your finances, it's no different. Connecting with other military families who understand the unique challenges you face can make all the difference in achieving your financial goals. By surrounding yourself with people who encourage, advise, and share their experiences, you'll find the motivation and wisdom to continue growing financially —no matter what obstacles come your way.

This chapter is all about the importance of building and nurturing a **supportive community** that will help you stay on track and reach your financial potential. Whether you're looking for financial advice, accountability, or just someone to encourage you when things get tough, building this network is a crucial step on your financial journey.

Connecting with Other Military Families for Financial Advice and Encouragement

The beauty of being part of the military community is that you're never truly alone. Other military families are walking the same path as you—dealing with moves, deployments, and juggling family life with service life. Many of them have learned financial lessons the hard way and are eager to share their insights, tips, and strategies with others.

- **Learning from Shared Experiences:**
  Every military family has unique stories and experiences, especially when it comes to managing finances. Some may have navigated deployments while maintaining financial stability, others may have successfully bought homes despite frequent moves, or built significant savings on a tight budget. By sharing these stories, you can gain insights into what's worked for others and apply those strategies to your own situation.

- **Financial Accountability and Motivation:**
  It's easy to lose momentum when you're working on your own financial goals. Connecting with others can provide you with **accountability** and encouragement. Whether it's through regular

check-ins, group challenges, or simply sharing milestones, a community can help you stay focused and motivated when life gets challenging.

- **The Power of Collective Knowledge:**
  You don't have to reinvent the wheel. Other families have faced the same challenges and figured out solutions. By connecting with them, you can avoid common mistakes, save time, and learn new strategies to optimize your financial plan. Whether it's tips on saving during a PCS, using military benefits effectively, or navigating the Thrift Savings Plan (TSP), you can find valuable advice from those who have already walked the path.

Using Online Forums, Local Groups, and Professional Networks

While your military base and local community are invaluable resources, the digital world offers even more opportunities to connect. Online forums, social media groups, and professional networks can all provide access to a wealth of knowledge and resources.

- **Online Forums:**
  Websites like Military.com, Reddit's military threads, and other dedicated forums provide a space for military families to ask questions, share experiences, and offer advice. These communities

are especially helpful for getting quick answers to pressing financial questions or learning from others' successes and failures.

- **Social Media Groups:**
  Facebook groups, Instagram pages, and Twitter accounts focused on military families are great places to connect with others in real-time. Many groups are dedicated specifically to military finances, offering financial tips, investment strategies, and advice on how to maximize benefits. Follow influencers who share military-related financial content, or participate in live Q&A sessions to learn more from experts.

- **Professional Networks:**
  Don't forget the power of professional organizations dedicated to military families, like the **National Military Family Association (NMFA)**, or organizations that offer career services and mentorship. These groups can connect you to professionals who can guide your financial journey, offer career advancement advice, or help you network as you transition to civilian life.

Exercise: Reach Out to One Resource or Group to Expand Your Support System

Building a supportive community starts with **taking the first step**. Now, let's turn this chapter's insights into action. Here's your exercise:

1. **Identify a Resource or Group**
   Think about which type of community would benefit you most. It could be a local group at your base, an online forum, a financial expert who works with military families, or a professional networking group. **Choose one resource** or group that feels like a good fit.

2. **Make the Connection**
   Reach out and introduce yourself! Don't be shy—whether it's a comment on a social media post, a question in an online forum, or sending an email to a professional, making the initial connection is crucial. Remember, everyone has been where you are and is eager to offer help and guidance.

3. **Engage and Participate**
   Once you've connected, be proactive in engaging. Ask questions, share your own experiences, and contribute to the discussions. The more you invest in the community, the more you'll get back. Don't hesitate to share your own financial successes, ask for advice when you hit a roadblock, and offer encouragement to others.

4. **Set a Goal to Stay Connected**
   Create a plan to regularly check in with your chosen community. Whether it's setting aside time once a week to read posts and offer feedback or scheduling a monthly call with a mentor, staying connected will provide continuous support throughout your financial journey.

Conclusion:

Building a supportive community around your financial goals isn't just about advice—it's about motivation, encouragement, and knowing that you're not alone. Connecting with fellow military families can help you navigate the challenges of military life, learn from others, and find the support you need to keep pushing forward. Remember, your **financial success** is a journey that you don't have to walk alone.

In the next chapter, we'll wrap everything up and help you create an **actionable roadmap** for your financial future. Keep building that community, stay motivated, and keep moving forward—your future is waiting!

Chapter 18
Celebrating Progress and Adjusting Goals

Throughout your journey toward financial stability and success, it's essential to pause and **celebrate your progress**. In the hustle of managing military life, you can sometimes overlook the small wins that add up to major achievements. Celebrating milestones, big or small, helps maintain motivation, boosts morale, and reinforces the positive financial habits you've worked so hard to establish.

This chapter is about taking time to acknowledge your growth, adjusting your goals as your life evolves, and continuing to move forward with purpose and energy. The journey doesn't end with achieving one goal; it's about continual growth and celebration of the progress you make along the way. Let's dive into the importance of reflecting on your success and adjusting your plans to keep thriving.

The Importance of Acknowledging Milestones, No Matter How Small

Many military families are so focused on the next move, the next deployment, or the next goal that they forget to look back and celebrate how far they've come. Every step forward—whether it's saving your first $500, paying off a credit card, or successfully setting up a new budget after a PCS—deserves recognition. Here's why celebrating progress matters:

- **Motivation to Keep Going:**
  Acknowledging your achievements—no matter how small—serves as a powerful reminder that you **are making progress**. Even if your financial goals seem far off, the small victories you accumulate along the way are proof that you're headed in the right direction. Celebrating each milestone helps build momentum and reinforces the habit of persistence.

- **Boosting Morale:**
  Military life is filled with ups and downs, and it's easy to get discouraged. Recognizing your accomplishments helps keep spirits high, especially during challenging times. It reminds you that you're capable, resilient, and making strides toward building a secure future for your family.

- **Strengthening Your Family's Bond:**
  When you celebrate together as a family, it's an opportunity to create a positive, shared experience. It's a reminder that your financial goals are not just about numbers—they're about creating a better life for the ones you love. Celebrating together can deepen your sense of unity and purpose.

Adjusting Financial Plans as Your Family Grows and Your Circumstances Change

Life in the military is ever-changing, and with those changes come **evolving financial needs**. As your family grows, as deployments happen, as you transition to civilian life, or as your financial situation improves, your financial goals may need to be updated. The key is to remain flexible and adaptable to the changes that arise.

- **Review and Reassess Regularly:**
  Just as your family's needs evolve, so should your financial plan. Make it a habit to regularly review your goals and update them as your circumstances change. Perhaps you've received a raise, or you're expecting a new addition to the family—these milestones call for a reevaluation of your financial priorities. What was a goal a year ago might need to be adjusted or refined to align with your current life situation.

- **Celebrating Progress While Adapting to Change:**
  Changing goals doesn't mean you're starting over; it's an opportunity to **grow** and **evolve**. Just as your family adapts to new assignments, new cities, and new challenges, so too should your financial plans. Whether it's increasing savings goals, shifting focus to debt repayment, or planning for future education costs, adjusting your plan is a natural part of the journey.

- **Embrace Flexibility:**
  Military life is unpredictable, and your financial plan should be able to accommodate the inevitable shifts that will occur. Being too rigid in your goals can lead to frustration and burnout when things don't go according to plan. Instead, embrace **flexibility** and treat financial planning as a dynamic process that grows with you and your family.

Exercise: Identify Three Recent Financial Wins and Celebrate Them with Your Family

Taking time to reflect on your progress is essential to maintaining motivation and perspective. For this exercise, let's focus on your recent **financial wins**. This could include anything from a successful move, reaching a savings milestone, or simply sticking to your budget during a tough month. It's about recognizing where you've succeeded!

1. **Identify Three Wins:**
   Think about the last few months and identify three financial wins. Perhaps you managed to avoid unnecessary spending during a PCS, paid off a portion of your debt, or made strides toward a long-term financial goal like retirement savings. No win is too small to count—every step forward is a victory.

2. **Celebrate as a Family:**
   Take a moment to **celebrate** with your family. This could be as simple as sharing the news over dinner, taking a day trip to enjoy some downtime together, or even treating yourselves to a small indulgence—whatever feels like a meaningful way to acknowledge your hard work. The goal is to honor the effort and commitment that led to these wins.

3. **Reflect on the Journey:**
   Reflect on the lessons learned during this part of your journey. What strategies or habits helped you reach these milestones? Celebrate the process just as much as the results. This celebration is not just about the outcome, but about acknowledging the

dedication, discipline, and perseverance that made it possible.

Conclusion:

Remember, the journey to financial success is **ongoing**. Life will continue to throw curveballs, but the way you handle them—by celebrating your wins and adjusting your goals—will shape your long-term success. Your financial milestones are a testament to your resilience, discipline, and determination.

As your family grows, your goals evolve, and your circumstances change, don't forget to take the time to celebrate your progress. You're not just building financial stability; you're building a legacy for your future. Keep adjusting, keep growing, and most importantly, keep celebrating—because every step forward is a victory worth acknowledging.

In the next chapter, we'll wrap up everything you've learned and provide an actionable plan for continuing your journey to financial freedom. Keep up the hard work, and don't forget to celebrate your success along the way!

Conclusion
A Financially Strong Military Family

As we close this journey through the essentials of military family finance, it's important to reflect on the key lessons you've learned and the powerful steps you can take to ensure your family's financial success. From managing frequent moves to maximizing the benefits and resources available to you, you now have a clearer picture of how to build a financially secure future, no matter what challenges military life brings.

Recap of Key Lessons: Flexibility, Planning, and Leveraging Unique Benefits

One of the most important takeaways from this book is the need for **flexibility**. Military life is inherently unpredictable, and while you can't control everything, you **can control** how you respond. By building a flexible financial plan, you're setting yourself up to thrive no matter the circumstances. Remember that a budget is not a rigid structure but a living document that adjusts as your life changes. The more adaptable you are, the more resilient your family's finances will be.

Planning is another cornerstone of your financial strength. You've learned to set clear, actionable goals—both short-term and long-term—and how to adjust them when necessary. You've created a budget that works for your family, identified ways to save and grow your money, and even planned for retirement through the Thrift Savings Plan. With consistent planning and intentional action, you can weather the storms of military life and emerge stronger on the other side.

Finally, **leveraging your unique military benefits** is a powerful tool that can help you achieve financial security faster than you might expect. From the Thrift Savings Plan to military discounts, to programs like Military OneSource and the GI Bill, you have access to a wealth of resources designed to help you thrive. By using these benefits wisely and consistently, you're setting yourself up for financial success that extends beyond your service.

Encouragement to Take the Next Steps Today

The most important lesson of all is that your **journey toward financial freedom begins now**. You have all the tools, strategies, and resources you need to start building a secure financial future. It's time to take action, whether it's reviewing your budget, setting up an emergency fund, or opening an investment account. The steps may seem small at first, but they add up quickly, and the momentum you create today will fuel your financial progress for years to come.

Don't wait for the "perfect" time to start—because the perfect time is always right now. Whether you're just starting to save or planning for retirement, every action you take brings you closer to your goal. The strength of your family's financial foundation depends on the choices you make today.

Final Call to Action: Use the Tools and Strategies in This Book to Build a Secure Financial Future

You've made it this far, and now it's time to use the tools and strategies in this book to **take control** of your financial future. The blueprint for success is in your hands. Whether you're budgeting, saving, investing, or planning for the future, know that each decision you make is a step toward building the life you want for yourself and your loved ones.

Remember, you are **not alone** in this journey. There are resources, communities, and support systems available to help guide you along the way. Reach out, connect, and keep learning. Every step you take towards financial security is a victory for your family, and with each new goal you achieve, you're not just securing your own future—you're setting a legacy for generations to come.

Stay committed. Stay focused. And most importantly, stay **inspired**. Financial strength doesn't happen overnight, but with perseverance and intentionality, you can create a future filled with peace, security, and freedom.

The time to take action is now—so let's get started on building the financially strong military family you deserve!

Your journey begins today—embrace it, and watch your financial dreams become reality.

www.ingramcontent.com/pod-product-compliance
Lightning Source LLC
Chambersburg PA
CBHW050259230526
45471CB00005B/1952